STUDY GUIDE
Dennis Werner

6TH
EDITION

Cultural
Anthropology

Carol R. Ember
Hunter College of the City University of New York
Human Relations Area Files

Melvin Ember
Human Relations Area Files

PRENTICE HALL, ENGLEWOOD CLIFFS, NEW JERSEY 07632

Editorial/production supervision and
interior design: **Renata Slauter**
Manufacturing buyer: **Ed O'Dougherty**

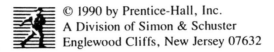
Printed in the United States of America

10 9 8 7 6 5 4 3 2 1

ISBN 0-13-168451-5

Prentice-Hall International (UK) Limited, *London*
Prentice-Hall of Australia Pty. Limited, *Sydney*
Prentice-Hall Canada Inc., *Toronto*
Prentice-Hall Hispanoamericana, S.A., *Mexico*
Prentice-Hall of India Private Limited, *New Delhi*
Prentice-Hall of Japan, Inc., *Tokyo*
Simon & Schuster Asia Pte. Ltd., *Singapore*
Editora Prentice-Hall Do Brasil, Ltda., *Rio de Janeiro*

Contents

v

To the Student

This Study Guide is designed to help you understand the material in the sixth edition of *Cultural Anthropology* by Carol R. Ember and Melvin Ember. After reading a chapter in the text, consult the corresponding chapter in this guide to help you organize your thoughts and review the material. Each Study Guide chapter has six parts: 1) a chapter outline, 2) an overview, 3) common misunderstandings, 4) key terms and concepts, 5) review questions, and 6) study questions.

Chapter Outline

The chapter outline shows you visually how each chapter is organized. Look first at the main headings (in large roman numerals). This will show you at a glance the main points of the chapter. Then examine the sub-listings for each main heading. If you can visualize how the text chapter is organized you will find it much easier to remember things because you will understand *why* points were discussed at different points in the chapter.

Overview

The overview summarizes the text chapter's main points. As you read through the overview, question yourself about each point. Do you understand the arguments provided to explain different phenomena? Can you give examples to illustrate each point?

Common Misunderstandings

The text attempts to be as clear as possible, but students often continue to misunderstand important points. This section anticipates some of the most common misconceptions students have regarding anthropology. When reading this section, make sure you understand not only what the common misconception is, but also *why* it is wrong.

Key Terms and Concepts

The key terms and concepts section contains important terminology introduced in the chapter. Try to define the term, being careful to distinguish it from related terms when necessary. If you find a word or expression you do not understand, check the glossary at the end of the textbook. If you cannot find the term there, then go back to the page in the text chapter where the expression is introduced.

Review Questions

This section of the Study Guide contains a variety of objective questions: fill-in, multiple choice, and matching questions. These items can help you test how well you have understood the main points of the text chapter.

Read each question carefully and write your answer in the blanks provided, or else circle the correct letter choice. Make sure you read through all of the alternative answers to multiple choice questions. It is sometimes more important to understand why a given answer is wrong than to remember the correct answer itself. When you have finished answering all of the questions in the chapter, check your responses with the correct answers provided at the end of each Study Guide chapter. If any of your answers are incorrect, return to the text page listed in parentheses after the question, and review the material related there.

Study Questions

The study questions are essay questions similar to those you might be asked in class discussions or on an exam. Read the questions, think about them and perhaps jot down notes or make a brief outline of the points to cover in your answer. It is a good idea to take a few minutes to do this for every chapter while the material covered is still fresh in your mind.

If you go through each of these study and review aids after you read each text chapter, you will be better prepared to participate in class discussions and clarify those points you did not understand. You will also be more prepared to apply what you have learned to the following chapters. Briefly skimming the chapter outlines and chapter overviews before an exam will refresh your memory and help you organize your thoughts.

Cultural Anthropology

What is Anthropology?

Chapter Outline

I. The scope of anthropology

II. The holistic approach

III. The anthropological curiosity

IV. Fields of anthropology
   A. Physical anthropology
   B. Cultural anthropology
     1. Archeology
     2. Anthropological linguistics
     3. Ethnology

V. The usefulness of anthropology

Overview

This chapter introduces the field of anthropology. It shows 1) how anthropology is different from other disciplines, 2) how different kinds of anthropologists carry out their work, and 3) how anthropology can be useful.

The word anthropology comes from the Greek words for "man" and "study," and refers literally to the study of humans. But unlike other academic fields that also study humans, anthropology has three characteristics that distinguish it as a separate discipline. First, anthropology is *BROADER* in scope than other fields. That is, anthropologists are interested in people living in all the far corners of the world and at all times -- from the earliest humans to evolve up to the present. They are even interested in non-human primates for the light they can shed on human nature. Second, anthropology is also *HOLISTIC*. This means that anthropologists are interested in everything about humans -- from their biological characteristics, to their physical environment, their psychological make-ups and their religious beliefs. Third, anthropology is interested in *TYPICAL* traits. That is, anthropologists want to know *why* some cultures are different from others in such features as their marriage customs, economic systems, languages, or artistic styles.

Not all anthropologists can study everything, of course, so most anthropologists specialize in their research. One common division separates anthropologists into four main sub-fields -- physical anthropology, archeology, anthropological linguistics and ethnology. These last three are grouped together as CULTURAL ANTHROPOLOGY. PHYSICAL ANTHROPOLOGISTS attempt to answer two basic types of questions: 1) How did humans and their social organization evolve? and

2) Why do contemporary humans vary biologically? To answer questions about evolution *paleontologists* study the fossil remains of the ancestors of our species, homo sapiens, and *primatologists* examine the lifestyles of different species of non-human primates (prosimians, monkeys and apes) that share a common past with homo sapiens. To understand why humans vary biologically, physical anthropologists draw upon the work of human geneticists, population biologists, and epidemiologists. ARCHEOLOGISTS study the remains of past cultures in order to answer such questions as why plants were first domesticated or why civilizations first arose. In their excavations they look for such things as broken pottery, stone tools or ancient garbage heaps that can give them information about how people lived. ANTHROPOLOGICAL LINGUISTS study various aspects of language, and usually work with unwritten languages. *Historical linguists* look at the changes in language over time. They may discover whether certain contemporary languages had a common ancestor and, if so, when they diverged. *Descriptive linguists* are interested in discovering the rules that determine how words and sounds are put together in different languages. *Sociolinguists* study the different ways people talk in varying contexts. ETHNOLOGISTS study the ways people think and act in different societies. *Ethnographers* spend long periods of time living with the people in a culture in order to describe their lives. *Ethnohistorians* examine the written documents left by missionaries, explorers and government officials in order to reconstruct a group's history. *Cross-cultural researchers* use the available information on different societies in order to find out why some societies have a given typical characteristic while others do not.

Anthropology is useful for several reasons. First, it can help us understand why humans behave the way they do. The more we learn about ourselves, the more likely we will be able to solve some of our social problems. Second, anthropology can also help us avoid misunderstandings about people who are different from ourselves. Third, anthropology can give us a sense of humility and of accomplishment by placing our own culture in perspective with the vast history of human existence, exposing our own vulnerabilities and strengths.

Common Misunderstandings

Movies and popular magazines often give the impression that most anthropologists spend their time digging for fossil bones or living among exotic primitive cultures. While some anthropologists do these kinds of fieldwork, students should be aware that anthropology is much broader in scope. Today most anthropologists do their fieldwork in "civilized" societies rather than among primitive peoples, and many do most of their research in libraries.

Another common misperception is that anthropologists are concerned primarily with describing other cultures. Actually, most anthropologists are more interested in making comparisons in order to *explain differences*, rather than simply describe them. There is also some confusion about what the purpose of anthropology should be. While some anthropologists are deeply involved in the plight of specific minority peoples around the world, most anthropologists see their research as more important for our general understanding of humanity.

Key Terms and Concepts

anthropology

anthropological linguistics

archeology

cultural anthropology

descriptive linguistics

ethnography

ethnohistory

ethnology

historical linguistics

holistic

human paleontology

human variation

physical anthropology

primatology

sociolinguistics

typical traits

Review Questions

1. Compared to earlier years, today's anthropology (2)
a. concentrates more on how humans evolved.
b. is seen as a subfield of sociology.
c. is more limited in scope.
d. is more concerned with tribal cultures.
e. overlaps more with other academic fields.

2. Anthropological studies often overlap with those of (2-5)
a. sociology.
b. biology.
c. human genetics.
d. psychology.
e. all of the above.

3. One of the reasons why American Blacks, American Indians, Orientals and
   Southern Europeans often refuse to drink fresh milk is that (2-3)
a. traditional religious beliefs among these people defined milk as taboo.
b. they are all too poor to buy milk products.
c. their ancestors were accustomed to diets rich in meats which made them snub
   dairy products.
d. they often lack the enzyme needed to digest fresh milk.
e. both a and d are correct.

4. Because anthropologists are interested in all areas of human experience, we
say they use a(n)_____ approach. (3)

5. Anthropologists study all of the following *except* (3)
a. monkeys and apes.
b. technologically advanced societies.
c. the ways people use language.
d. dinosaur anatomy.
e. past cultures.

6. Compared to other social scientists, anthropologists (2-3)
a. enjoy more respect in the academic community.
b. are interested in more aspects of human life.
c. are interested in a broader range of human cultures.
d. are more likely to compare the "typical" traits of different cultures.
e. Answers b, c and d are correct.

7. The two main subfields of anthropology are_____ and _____(4)

8. Most physical anthropologists study (4)
a. exercise techniques that might help those in our society stay more fit.
b. the natural forces (gravity, electromagnetism and "weak" forces) that affect human technologies.
c. the physical environments from which different peoples extract their living.
d. how humans evolved, and how human populations differ biologically today.
e. all of the above.

9. Human paleontologists depend on data from (4)
a. vertebrate paleontology.
b. comparative anatomy.
c. geology.
d. comparative primate studies.
e. all of the above.

10. Physical anthropologists are particularly interested in studying the chimpanzee because (4)
a. chimpanzees have mating customs similar to humans.
b. chimpanzees are the most abundant primate.
c. the evolutionary record suggests that humans evolved from chimpanzees.
d. studies of blood chemistry suggest that chimpanzees are very closely related to modern humans.
e. all of the above.

11. We know that all humans alive today belong to the same species because (5)
a. they all have the same genes.
b. they all have the same blood type.
c. they all evolved from the same ancestor.
d. they all can interbreed successfully.
e. Humans do *not* all belong to the same species.

12. In using the term "culture," anthropologists are referring to a society's (5)
a. system of social stratification.
b. cultivated foods.
c. music, literature and art.
d. typical disease agents.
e. Answers a,b and c are correct.

13. Compared to historians, archeologists (5)
a. are less interested in artwork.
b. often study societies that date back more than 5000 years ago.
c. are more interested in societies with written records.
d. get more of their information from such buried remains as garbage heaps.
e. Answers b and d are correct.

14. Which of the following is an archeologist *unlikely* to use for information about a society that existed 7000 years ago? (5-6)
a. written records of trade goods.
b. stone tools.

c. an ancient garbage heap.
d. broken bits of pottery.
e. pollen.

15. The study of how people actually speak in different contexts is called_____. (7)

16. In order to reconstruct the history of an unwritten language, historical linguists (7)
a. rely heavily on those few moments in the past when people left a pictorial record of the group.
b. can compare contemporary related languages to find out what features may have been ancestral to them all.
c. must rely on early records left by visitors to a society.
d. often use artwork and other "indirect" indicators of a group's language.
e. Historical linguists cannot reconstruct a past language without a written record.

17. Compared to ethnologists, ethnographers (7)
a. are more likely to study ethnic groups within a contemporary society rather than faraway "primitive" cultures.
b. spend more effort on describing a particular culture.
c. are more likely to study societies with written languages.
d. spend more time analyzing why societies in different parts of the world vary in their customs.
e. Answers a and d are correct.

18. The _____ investigates written documents about non-literate cultures in order to discover how a particular culture has changed over time. (8)

Match the following questions with the type of specialist who would most likely be able to answer them.
a. Are there different ways of talking to high-status and low-status people?
b. How did agriculture begin?
c. What did the ancestors to modern humans look like?
d. Why do people in some societies, but not others, have more than one wife?
e. How do chimpanzees behave in the wild?

19. Primatologist_____ (5)
20. Sociolinguist_____(7)
21. Archeologist_____(6)
22. Human paleontologist_____(4)
23. Cross-cultural researcher_____ (8)

Study Questions

1. What do anthropologists mean when they say their field is "holistic"? Can all anthropologists study everything?

2. How is anthropology different from such fields as psychology, sociology, or biology?

3. What kinds of questions do physical anthropologists ask and what kinds of information do they examine to answer these questions?

4. What kinds of information do human paleontologists, historical linguists, archeologists and ethnohistorians use to reconstruct the past? What kinds of questions are they likely to answer about this past?

5. In what ways might anthropology be useful in avoiding misunderstandings between people of different cultures?

6. Describe the kinds of questions that interest each of the four main subdivisions of anthropology: physical anthropology, archeology, anthropological linguistics and ethnology.

Answers to Review Questions

1)e; 2)e; 3)d; 4)holistic; 5)d; 6)e; 7)physical anthropology and cultural anthropology; 8)d; 9)e; 10)d; 11)d; 12)e; 13)e; 14)a; 15)sociolinguistics; 16)b; 17)b; 18)ethnohistorian; 19)e; 20)a; 21)b; 22)c; 23)d

The Concept of Culture

Chapter Outlines

Overview

This chapter introduces the concept of culture and shows its importance in anthropological research. It begins by emphasizing the importance of cultural relativism -- the idea that another culture should be understood in the context of that society's problems and opportunities. Cultural relativism is hindered by ethnocentrism (the tendency to judge another culture in terms of our own), and by the myth of the "noble savage" (the romanticizing of another culture).

The term *culture* refers to innumerable aspects of life, including behaviors, beliefs, attitudes and values. To be considered cultural a trait must be commonly shared by others and must be learned. Individual idiosyncrasies and genetically inherited traits are not cultural. By this definition some other species such as monkeys and apes also possess cultures. Unlike other animals, however, humans possess a symbolic language which allows us to transmit our cultures verbally, without having to demonstrate every belief, attitude or behavior. The term *society* traditionally refers to a group of people occupying a particular territory and speaking a common language.

In order to describe a culture, anthropologists must focus on customary behavior rather than on individual variations. This focus is possible, in part, because cultural constraints limit the range of individual behavior within any society. Direct constraints involve the use of force to ensure conformity. Indirect constraints discourage non-conformity by such means as ridicule or social isolation. Still there is much room for individuality because the *ideals* of a society (the ideas about how people *ought* to behave) do not always conform to the ways people actually behave or want to behave . In order to discover cultural patterns, anthropologists sometimes rely on frequency distributions in order to distinguish the modal response (a statistical term referring to the most frequent behavior, belief or attitude encountered). In order to save time in determining the modal response, researchers can often rely on a random sample -- a sample in which each case has an equal chance to be chosen.

Anthropologists generally assume that most cultural traits are adaptive, integrated and ever-changing. Adaptive cultural traits are those that enhance the chances that the culture will survive within its particular environment. For example, a long postpartum sex taboo is adaptive in societies with low protein supplies because it ensures that women will be able to nurse their infants on protein-rich milk for several years before becoming pregnant again. In other societies such a taboo might not be adaptive because it would limit the number of children a woman could bear. Because one cultural trait can affect another, cultural traits must generally be compatible with one another. That is culture is usually *integrated*. Because social and physical environments change constantly, cultural traits, if they are to remain adaptive and integrated, must also change constantly.

Common Misunderstandings

Reading accounts of exotic cultures often gives students the impression that cultural traits are completely arbitrary, and that they could be adopted by our own society if we simply liked them enough. This may be true for some cultural traits (like buttons on men's jacket cuffs) which have little importance for adaptation or for cultural integration. However, most traits could not so easily be grafted onto our own culture, because most cultural features are attuned to specific environmental and social needs that may not be the same as our own.

Another common misunderstanding is that "culture" refers to "tradition" passed along from parents to offspring. Actually, many cultures develop outside of familial surroundings. The fact that societies are always changing implies that people may come to share new behaviors, beliefs or values that they pick up from each other during their lives. Many subcultures have this characteristic -- such as the subculture of a business corporation, of "poverty," of a prison or of a drug-using community.

Key Terms and Concepts

adaptive traits
cultural constraints
cultural relativism
culture
ethnocentrism
frequency distribution
ideal cultural patterns
integrated traits

kwashiorkor
language
maladaptive traits
mode
"noble savage"
random distribution
society
subculture

Review Questions

1. The anthropological attitude that a society's customs and ideals should be viewed in the context of that society's problems and opportunities is called _____. (15)

2. Ethnocentrism refers to (15)
a. the need to focus on another society's problems.
b. the judging of another culture in terms of one's own.
c. the view that other societies are better than one's own.
d. the tendency of people of the same ethnic background to group together.
e. the tendency for people to base their behavior on the ideal "pattern" of their culture.

3. The tendency to romantically idealize simpler cultures is called the _____ view. (16)

4. One reason anthropologists avoid the "noble savage" view is that (16)
a. it is based on romantic appeal, not objective understanding.
b. it is based on a mistaken notion that primitives may have more desireable traits than more advanced cultures.
c. this view is associated with some of the most exploitative actions civilized societies have perpetrated on native peoples.
d. it often degrades primitive people in the public eye, reducing them to a brutish nature.
e. aristocracies have generally not been found in primitive cultures.

5. In anthropology the term "culture" refers to (17)
a. traits, both biological and learned, that are shared by a population.
b. the "finer things in life" as these are seen by people of different societies.
c. the learned behaviors, values, attitudes and beliefs shared by members of a group.
d. the symbolic aspects of life in a society -- including beliefs, values and attitudes, but not necessarily behaviors.
e. the ideals of a society.

6. For something to be considered cultural it must be (17)
a. commonly shared.
b. flexible.
c. accepted as legitimate by a society.
d. instinctive.
e. symbolic.

7. Which of the following is *not* an example of a cultural pattern? (18)
a. the ways people get their food in a society
b. the modal natural hair color of a population
c. the musical tastes of people in a society
d. the washing of sweet potatoes by Japanese monkeys
e. the languages spoken in a society

8. Which of the following statements is most true? (18)
a. Culture is learned.
b. Culture is not influenced by instincts.
c. Only humans have culture
d. Culture is genetically based.
e. For culture to exist, there must be symbolic language.

9. One of the differences between human cultural behavior and that of monkeys and apes is that (18)
a. a great deal of human culture is learned through language.
b. humans learn their culture.
c. humans do not have instinctual behaviors.
d. apes and monkeys do not change their culture over time.
e. apes and monkeys do not have culture.

10. In contrast to other forms of communication found in other animals, humans' symbolic language (18)
a. can be used to communicate about things that are not present.
b. can be used to communicate about things through sounds.
c. can change from one generation to another.
d. can be used to express emotional states.
e. is learned.

11. Traditionally, anthropologists have dealt with the cultures of (19)
a. different ethnic groups.
b. different socioeconomic groups.
c. different animals.
d. different occupational groups.
e. different societies.

12. To deal with individual variations, anthropologists generally (20)
a. limit themselves to observing only a few prominent people in any given society.
b. try to describe everything they see people do around them.
c. describe ideals rather than actual behavior.
d. focus on the range of customary behaviors.
e. focus on a few selected individuals who can "represent" a group.

13. American dancing is an example of (20)
a. a behavior that allows for great variation, but also has its cultural limits on variation.
b. a behavior that is not culturally patterned
c. a cultural trait that is not adaptive.
d. a behavior that is probably universal to all human societies.
e. a cultural trait that is not integrated.

14. Indirect cultural constraints refer to (22)
a. cultural limitations on variation that are not obligatory but that are generally accepted to avoid ridicule or other problems.
b. situations in which third parties, like policemen, intervene to make people conform to cultural ideals.

c. the psychological problems that occur when people try too hard to follow cultural norms.
d. situations in which people from other cultures find themselves suddenly obliged to follow local customs.
e. limitations on behavior that are determined by more powerful foreign culture and implemented via rules made by members of one's own group.

15. Studies of conformity in our own society show that (22)
a. people deliberately try to avoid conformity when asked to give their opinions on a matter.
b. people rarely conform to the opinions of others if they think their initial views are disputed.
c. people consistently misinterpret the opinions of others when these disagree with their own opinions.
d. people easily change their opinions to conform to the group when the group as a whole disagrees.
e. Americans are generally more independent and individualistic than other people.

16. Ideal cultural patterns (23)
a. are rarely reinforced through cultural constraints.
b. are more likely to be found in highly evolved societies.
c. are inevitably adaptive.
d. may be outmoded.
e. are more common in simpler societies than in complex ones.

17. Compared to Arabs, Americans (23)
a. generally stand closer to each other while conversing.
b. generally stand farther away from each other while conversing.
c. are more rigid about how far away they stand from each other while conversing.
d. are more flexible about how far away they stand from each other while conversing.
e. are less likely to be offended by the standing distances considered normal in other cultures.

Match the term with the description that fits it best.
a. the normal shape of a frequency-distribution.
b. a group in which each member has an equal chance of being selected.
c. the numerically most commonly encountered response in a frequency-distribution.
d. views about how people ought to behave and think

18. mode _____(23)
19. random sample_____(24)
20. ideal cultural pattern_____(23)
21. a bell-curve_____(23)

22. To determine the mode, an anthropologist is most likely to (23)
a. listen to sermons or lectures to discover a society's ideals.
b. consult knowledgeable experts.
c. act firmly, but not arrogantly, while presenting the new mode.

d. plot the frequency distribution of some trait.

e. think deeply about how people must be interpreting their lives.

23. A random sample is a sample (24)

a. in which each case has an equal chance of being chosen.

b. based on whichever cases happen to appear.

c. which cannot serve to represent the whole.

d. in which the categories of interest to the researcher are filled.

e. used to date materials based on the number of rans they emit per second.

24. A culturally adaptive trait (24-25)

a. may not be adaptive in all situations.

b. is unlikely to change over the years.

c. is a trait that is morally good in a given society.

d. is a trait that has evolved through biological evolution to adjust the individual.

e. is one that is flexible.

25. Cross-cultural studies suggest that a taboo on sex after a baby has been born may be adaptive in societies (25)

a. with limited protein supplies, in order to permit mothers to nurse their young for a longer period of time.

b. with more men than women, so that the men do not overburden the women with their sexual demands.

c. with a high incidence of venereal disease.

d. where men and women sleep in hammocks, in order to protect babies from being crushed by their parents.

e. where marriages are unstable.

26. Because cultures are composed of elements that are compatible with one another anthropologists say cultures are generally (27)

a. static.

b. adaptive.

c. maladaptive.

d. changing.

e. integrated.

Study Questions

1. How do anthropologists define "culture," "subculture" and "society?" Give examples of each.

2. How are human cultures different from those of other animals?

3. What are the differences between ideal and actual cultures? Why are they different?

4. What do anthropologists mean by the terms "random sample," "bell-shaped curve" and "mode"? What roles do these play in studying culture?

5. What do anthropologists mean when they say that culture is "adaptive?" Give examples. How is adaptation related to culture change and cultural integration?

Answers to Review Questions

1)cultural relativism; 2)b; 3)"noble savage"; 4)a; 5)c; 6)a; 7)b; 8)a; 9)a; 10)a; 11)e; 12)d; 13)a; 14)a; 15)d; 16)d; 17)b; 18)c; 19)b; 20)d; 21)a; 22)d; 23)a; 24)a; 25)a; 26)e

Chapter 3

Schools of Thought
in Cultural Anthropology

Chapter Outline

I. Theoretical orientations
 A. Early evolutionism
 B. Historical particularism
 C. Diffusionism
 D. Functionalism
 E. Structural Functionalism
 F. Psychological approaches
 G. Later evolutionism
 H. Structuralism
 I. Ethnoscience
 J. Cultural Ecology
 K. Political Economy
 L. Sociobiology

II. Subject and method orientations

III. The hypothesis-testing orientation

Overview

Different anthropologists hold different opinions about how cultural phenomena should be explained. This chapter gives a summary of the major schools in anthropology (called theoretical orientations), and points out some of their strengths and weaknesses.

Evolutionists, like Tylor and Morgan, disagreed with the view, prevalent in their day, that groups like American Indians were degenerated peoples. They argued that all cultures pass through the same stages, from the simple to the complex. American Indians were simply located at a lower level of cultural evolution than Europeans, but could eventually progress to the European level. Morgan argued that societies evolved from "hordes" living in promiscuity, through polygyny, to monogamous relationships. These early evolutionary ideas depended on weak evidence, including the notion of "survivals," customs that persist in more advanced societies, but are representative of early stages. Marx and Engels adopted Morgan's scheme of evolution and expanded it to include a future utopian state of communism, making Morgan a revered intellectual figure in the Soviet Union.

Historical particularists like Franz Boas rejected the use of poor data by evolutionary theorists and urged instead the collection of better data before attempting to arrive at generalizations. By emphasizing minute details, Boas' approach discouraged the formulation of explanations for why cultures vary.

1 4

Diffusionists argued that people are basically uninventive and explained cultural variation by claiming that traits were borrowed from other societies. British diffusionists thought most aspects of high civilizations diffused from Egypt. German and Austrian diffusionists suggested that there were a number of different cultural areas from which traits diffused. American diffusionists went beyond the German/Austrian school by proposing that researchers could determine which traits were oldest by examining which had diffused the farthest out from the center. Critics point out that diffusion cannot account for why societies chose to accept some of their neighbor's traits and reject others. Nor can it account for how the traits originated in the first place.

Functionalists, like Malinowski, explained cultural traits as serving to satisfy basic needs like food, sex, and relaxation. This view fails to explain why cultures vary, since specific cultural patterns may arise to fulfill a need that could be fulfilled just as easily by other means.

Structural functionalism, the school founded by Radcliffe-Brown, explains traits as existing to maintain the group's social structure. Critics argue that structural functionalism assumes at the outset that traits contribute to the maintenance of the social system, but it is possible that some traits in fact may undermine this system. Also, structural functionalism does not explain why other possible solutions were not adopted by a society.

Psychological anthropologists see certain cultural traits as arising from the psychological make-up of individuals. Early studies saw "national character" as arising from child-rearing practices. These studies were heavily criticized for using crude social science methods to substantiate *subjective* generalizations about personality differences between societies. Later studies attempted to explain differences in child-care patterns on the basis of factors like food-getting technologies or family composition. They also attempted to use personality differences to explain differences in certain aspects of culture like beliefs about illness.

Later evolutionists like White and Steward saw cultures as evolving into ever more complex forms that harness more energy per person per year. As with earlier evolutionists, White could not explain the details of cultural differences. Steward attempted to explain evolutionary details in specific societies by proposing a notion of multilinear evolution, in which some (but not all) societies pass through parallel sequences of development in order to adapt to particular environments. Unlike earlier evolutionists, Steward proposed a mechanism -- adaptation to particular environments -- to account for the evolution of particular societies.

Structuralism, as founded by Lévi-Strauss, sees culture as expressed in art, ritual and the details of daily life, as surface representations of the underlying structure of the human mind, in particular of the human tendency to organize things in terms of binary oppositions. This approach has been criticized as attempting to explain something that varies (human cultures) by reference to something that does not vary (the human mind). It is also viewed by many as being vague and untestable.

15

Ethnoscientists use techniques adopted from linguistics to discover the categories and rules that govern behavior within a society. They have been criticized for failing to explain why a society may develop a particular set of cultural rules in the first place.

Cultural ecologists try to explain cultural traits as being adapted to particular environments. Like functionalists, they have been criticized for failing to explain why societies develop one particular solution for a problem rather than other possible solutions.

Political economists explain how cultural traits are affected by the expansion of Western colonialism and the development of a world economic system. They emphasize the role of world history in determining local cultural characteristics.

Sociobiologists emphasize the role of natural selection, but, unlike evolutionists and cultural ecologists, they emphasize the role of individual selection in cultural evolution. They attempt to explain how cultural characteristics may be adaptive for individuals in a particular environment, and they emphasize the role of genes in cultural evolution.

Rather than identify with one of these theoretical orientations, some anthropologists identify themselves with a subject orientation (like economic anthropology, or cognitive anthropology), or with a method orientation (like cross-cultural research, or ethnohistory). Some anthropologists see themselves as having a "hypothesis-testing" orientation, in which explanations from many different theoretical orientations may be examined in order to test whether they agree with systematically collected data.

Common Misunderstandings

Many beginning students feel highly disturbed on discovering that academics have serious disagreements among themselves, not only over research results, but over more basic questions like: What is the goal of anthropology? How do we know that we know? What makes data reliable or not?

Some people react to this discovery by concluding that none of it really matters, and becoming indifferent to academic arguments, or even to life in general. Others decide uncritically to accept one position and reject all the others. Neither of these solutions is very good. We may never be able to decide which of the views is right, but we can at least try to understand the subtleness of the different points of view, even if we eventually decide to reject some of them.

Key Terms and Concepts

basic need
cognitive anthropology
cultural ecology
culture center
derived need

diffusionism
ethnoscience
evolutionists
fieldwork
functionalism

general evolution
group selection
historical particularism
individual selection
Kulturkreis
modal personality
multilinear evolution
participant observation
political economy
primary institution

secondary institution
sociobiology
specific evolution
structural functionalism
structuralism
survivals
symbolic anthropology
theoretical orientation
unilinear evolution
world-system

Review Questions

1. A general attitude about how cultural phenomena are to be explained is called a(n) _____ _____ in anthropology (32).

2. Which of the following beliefs did Tylor *not* hold? (32-33)
a. Because of their psychic similarities, people in different cultures find the same solutions to the same problems independently of each other.
b. American Indians are examples of people who degenerated from an earlier higher level.
c. Progress is possible for all.
d. Advanced cultures often have survivals from earlier levels of evolution.
e. Traits can spread from one society to another.

3. Morgan postulated that cultural patterns passed through an evolutionary sequence from (33)
a. patrilineality to matrilineality.
b. savage patrilocality to civilized bilocality.
c. a promiscuous horde to monogamy.
d. monogamy to more "open" marriages.
e. barbarism to savagery.

4. Marx and Engels extended Morgan's evolutionary scheme to include a future evolutionary stage characterized by (33)
a. state religions.
b. capitalism.
c. friendly cooperation between the different classes.
d. communism.
e. a tighter knit nuclear family.

5. Boas thought that anthropologists should (34)
a. try to uncover parallels in the ways different societies around the world adapted to their environments.
b. spend more time collecting data, and less time developing theories.
c. attempt to discover universal laws that might apply to all societies.
d. try to explain cultural variation by looking at the different ways people get their food.
e. compare similar cultural traits from different societies.

6. In contrast to the British diffusionists like Smith, Perry and Rivers, American diffusionists like Wissler (35-36)
a. believed it was possible to discover which traits were the oldest by examining which were farthest away from a cultural center.
b. thought all traits of advanced civilizations could be traced back to ancient Egypt.
c. did not attempt to analyze cultures by elaborating on "traits" divorced from their cultural context.
d. thought people were highly inventive.
e. were more interested in explaining why some cultures, but not others, adopted a given trait.

7. A weakness of diffusionist theories is that they (36)
a. do not explain why cultures accept, reject or modify the traits of their neighbors.
b. cannot explain cultural variation.
c. do not encourage anthropologists to collect new data.
d. foolishly attempt to explain why traits developed in the first place
e. pay little attention to the rich details about different societies.

8. According to Malinowski, social customs (36)
a. are playful expressions of the deep structures of human minds.
b. reflect the evolutionary stages of different societies.
c. function to satisfy the basic and derived needs of individuals in a society.
d. cannot be explained.
e. can be explained as forming part of a logistically consistent whole.

9. One problem with Malinowski's approach is that (36)
a. it encourages rapid and poorly carried out fieldwork projects.
b. it leads to relatively sterile accounts of a culture's social structure that do not take into account the desires of individuals.
c. it assumes that people are altruistic in sacrificing their own desires to the will of the group.
d. it cannot explain cultural differences because it uses universal needs to explain cultural traits that vary.
e. it is based on an evolutionary scheme that few people today would accept.

10. In contrast to Malinowski, Radcliffe-Brown (36-37)
a. thought social customs served primarily to maintain the social structure.
b. thought social customs served primarily to satisfy the needs of individuals, not of groups.
c. thought evolutionary schemes were helpful for understanding cultural variation.
d. explained customs like mother-in-law avoidance as resulting from child-rearing practices that create mistrust of unknown people.
e. emphasized the psychological aspect of cultural phenomena.

11. Studies carried out during World War II generally attributed "national character" (36)
a. to the different requirements for work in the different nations.
b. to differences in child-rearing practices.
c. to the warfare experiences of different countries in recent generations.

d. to the religions held by most of the people in a given country.
e. to the hard work and dedication of a country's people.

12. Cross-cultural studies of child-rearing show that (37)
a. the way children are brought up has little to do with the basic subsistence practices of their parents.
b. hunting and fishing societies tend to emphasize independence and self-reliance more than do agricultural societies.
c. parents in more primitive societies are generally less concerned about the welfare of their children.
d. people everywhere tend to stress the same personality characteristics in their children.
e. in most societies children are, in fact, not raised primarily by their parents, but by other kin.

13. In advocating a theory of multilinear evolution Steward argued that (38)
a. all societies evolve in the same invariable sequences.
b. comparisons between different cultures should await the collection of more solid data which place societal traits in their cultural context.
c. there may be sequences of parallel culture change in different areas.
d. it is impossible to make generalizations about how cultures evolve.
e. each society should be considered as having an evolutionary history all its own, and that historical "parallels" should be avoided as deceptive.

14. Lévi-Strauss' structuralist approach emphasizes (40-41)
a. the universality of binary oppositions in human thought and their expression in culture.
b. the logistics of social structure that makes different facets of a society compatible with one another.
c. those cultural traits that are common to some, but not all societies.
d. the evolutionary sequences that give rise to different social structures.
e. the human tendency to avoid intellectual challenges unless absolutely necessary.

15. Both ethnoscience and structuralism have been heavily influenced by (41)
a. descriptive linguistics.
b. evolutionary models from biology.
c. Keynesian economics.
d. behavioral psychology.
e. the development of statistical techniques.

16. The cultural ecologist tries to explain specific customs of a society by relating them to (42)
a. the language people speak.
b. particular aspects of the environment
c. child-rearing practices.
d. their origins in Egypt.
e. the universal needs of humans for food, shelter, love and sex.

17. Explanations of political economists generally emphasize (44)
a. the beneficent role of Western society on the economies of Third World countries.

b. the widely-varying political systems of different societies.
c. the effect of colonialism and the world-system on different cultures.
d. the ways underdeveloped nations attempt to swindle wealthier countries out of money.
e. the effects of a culture's internal structure in promoting cultural change.

18. In contrast to cultural ecology, sociobiology places more emphasis on (45)
a. group selection.
b. the role of the environment in shaping personality.
c. the ability of people to borrow traits from their neighbors.
d. individual selection.
e. the transmission of culture through language.

19. When anthropologists describe themselves as "economic anthropologists" they are referring to their (45)
a. subject orientation.
b. theoretical orientation.
c. interest in turning anthropology into a profitable business.
d. method orientation.
e. interest in adopting the techniques used by economists into anthropology.

20. People with an interest in hypothesis testing generally believe that (46)
a. all knowledge is uncertain.
b. arguments should be accepted on the basis of how logical and persuasive they appear.
c. empirical evidence is relatively unimportant in science.
d. scientific "progress" is impossible.
e. anthropologists should limit themselves to "interpreting" cultures rather than trying to explain cultural variation.

Study Questions

1. In what ways is Malinowski's emphasis on individual needs different from the the "culture and personality" approach?

2. What are the similarities and differences between the approaches of Malinowski and cultural ecology regarding the satisfaction of basic needs?

3. What are the differences in the ways Lévi-Strauss, ethnoscientists and the psychological anthropologists examine human mental behavior?

4. What are the differences in the views of early evolutionists, later evolutionists, and sociobiologists regarding cultural evolution?

5. What kinds of cultural traits could most easily be explained by cultural ecologists, political economists and psychological anthropologists? Explain.

Answers to Review Questions

1)theoretical orientation; 2)b; 3)c; 4)d; 5)b; 6)a; 7)a; 8)c; 9)d; 10)a; 11)b; 12)b; 13)c; 14)a; 15)a; 16)b; 17)c; 18)d; 19)a; 20)b

Explanation and Evidence

Chapter Outline

Overview

Although anthropologists are traditionally pictured as doing fieldwork in order to describe other cultures as accurately as possible, the ultimate goal of anthropology is not to describe, but to explain *why* people have certain traits or customs. This chapter shows how anthropologists generate and evaluate their explanations.

In science there are two kinds of explanation that researchers try to formulate -- associations and theories. Associations are statements of relationships between observable variables that allow us to predict what will happen in the future or imagine what has happened in the past. In the natural sciences, if the truth of an association is suggested by repeated observations we call the association a law. In the social sciences associations are usually probabilistic, and are called statistical associations. Theories attempt to explain the "why" of an association.

Where do theories come from? In part, they depend on sheer imagination; in part they may come from one's theoretical orientation which suggests which kinds of factors are most important. Some theories may come from analyses of a single case. Informants, for example, may themselves suggest reasons why they behave the way they do. Other theories may be inspired by comparing different societies and noting regularly occurring associations.

There may be many plausible theories to explain a given trait or custom. Because they contain elements, called theoretical constructs, that cannot be observed, theories cannot be proved. However, they can be disproved. Scientists attempt to reduce the number of potential explanations by making different predictions of what they would expect to find if each theory were correct. If the prediction for a given theory fails, then that theory is discarded as probably wrong. These predictions of what researchers expect to find are called hypotheses. They are usually predictions of expected associations.

In order to transform hypotheses into verifiable statements, researchers must provide operational definitions for each of the hypothesis' variables. That is, researchers must describe the procedure used to measure each variable. Measures may take the form of numbers on a scale, or they may simply be classifications, such as male and female, or French, German and American.

After deciding how to measure variables, researchers must next decide what sample of cases is to be investigated. From a list of cases to be sampled (known as a sampling universe) the researcher normally selects a random sample, in which each case has an equal chance to be selected. After measuring all the variables for each case, the researcher can then use statistical evaluation to see if the predicted associations are trustworthy. If the probability value of a statistical association is less than five times out of a hundred, then social scientists describe it as statistically significant, and may conclude that their theory is supported. Exceptions to the association may be due to measurement error, to other possible causes for the phenomenon, or to cultural lag.

Anthropologists collect different kinds of data. 1) Ethnographers engage in fieldwork to gather data by direct observation, or by asking questions of informants. Although most anthropological information ultimately comes from ethnographies, studies of single societies cannot easily test theories about cultural variation. 2) In nonhistorical controlled comparison, anthropologists compare ethnographic information obtained from a number of societies in a particular region. Such limited comparisons are useful not only for generating explanations, but also for testing them. 3) In cross-cultural research anthropologists make world-wide comparisons to test explanations about cultural variation. Conclusions drawn from such research have the advantage of being applicable to most societies. But cross-cultural research is limited in being able to examine only those explanations for which the required information is available. 4) In ethnohistorical research anthropologists analyze a single society at more than one point in time. Historical studies have the advantage of permitting researchers to demonstrate that presumed causes preceded their presumed effects. But historical research is limited in its dependence on second--hand data, and when using single societies, it cannot easily test hypotheses about cultural variation.

Common Misunderstandings

Many people have trouble understanding that explanations that are logical and plausible may still be wrong. As this chapter makes clear, even theories that sound good must be tested to see if they are consistent with data before we can accept them as trustworthy. We can never prove that a theory is correct, but can use testing procedures to sort out those theories that are definitely wrong from those theories that may be correct. Hypothesis testing, then, consists mostly of using empirical data to help us choose among alternative explanations of a phenomon.

It is also important to recognize that science is a *method*, not a final body of authoritative knowledge. In fact, by "disproving" but never "proving" ideas, the scientific method constantly questions authority.

Key Terms and Concepts

association
comparative study
contingency table
cross-cultural research
ethnography
ethnohistory
explanation
falsification
fieldwork
historical research
hypothesis
law
measure

nonhistorical controlled comparison
operational definition
probability value
random sample
sampling universe
single-case analysis
statistical association
statistically significant
tautology
tests of significance
theoretical construct
theory
variable

Review Questions

1. An explanation is an answer to (49)
a. a "how" question.
b. a "what" question.
c. a "who" question.
d. a "why" question.
e. a "when" question.

2. Explaining that a custom is due to tradition is problematic because (49)
a. traditions and customs are very different kinds of phenomena.
b. this amounts to a tautology.
c. anthropologists prefer "forward" thinking rather than fruitless reminiscing on the past.
d. cultures are always changing so that customs can never be "traditional."
e. people may invent new customs that have nothing to do with tradition.

3. A statement about the association between two observable variables whose truth is suggested by repeated observation is called a(n)_____(49).

4. Explanations of laws and statistical associations are called _____. (50)

5. In contrast to associations, theories (50)
a. are usually more complicated, containing a series of statements.
b. are generally simpler and more elegant.
c. are generally not very useful in science.

d. can be proved while associations cannot.

e. are unscientific because they have not been proved.

6. When scientists say that a theory is falsifiable, they mean that (51)

a. it results from misleading information that has been altered by unscrupulous scholars.

b. it is not very good because people could easily distort its meaning.

c. it can be discarded because it may well be wrong.

d. it can be tested to determine if it is wrong.

e. it is not worth examining because we know from prior research that it is wrong.

7. Which of the following statements is most correct? (51)

a. Theories can be proved, but hypotheses cannot.

b. Theories and hypotheses can be disproved.

c. Theories can be disproved, but hypotheses cannot.

d. Theories and hypotheses can be proved.

e. Hypotheses can be proved, but theories cannot.

8. Predictions of what might be found if a theory is correct are called _____ (51)

9. Theoretical orientations (52)

a. serve only to suggest procedures to test explanations already proposed by others.

b. can serve only as a guide, suggesting where to look for answers to questions.

c. suggest specific explanations to particular phenomena.

d. are used as the primary criterion to evaluate whether explanations are acceptable or not.

e. are generally recognized to have little relationship to theories.

10. One of the dangers in accepting an old and respected theory that has not been tested is that (52)

a. theories that are highly respected are usually suspect, because they tend to support unjust economic, political and social systems.

b. over time theories that were previously true eventually lose their value because people no longer believe in them.

c. age eventually wears away all things.

d. we may delude ourselves into thinking a question has already been solved when in fact it has not.

e. people change their minds about what kinds of explanations should be accepted. Clinging to older ideas may make us out of date.

11. An operational definition refers to (53)

a. a general definition that conveys the gist of what a researcher is trying to study.

b. a definition that allows us to dissect a phenomenon into its various parts.

c. an expression that appears in a theory.

d. a description of the procedure used to measure a variable.

e. the terms as they appear in a hypothesis.

12. In order for an association to be considered a law it must (53)
a. be approved by a local assembly.
b. be replicated by many different researchers.
c. be proven through the use of statistics.
d. be composed of members who have voluntarily agreed to associate themselves with the group.
e. be approved by an authoritative group of scientists.

13. Which of the following is *least likely* to be used as a measure in an anthropological study? (55)
a. classification of people according to country of birth.
b. temperature as read from a thermometer.
c. classification of competitors in a "three-legged" race according to who finished first and who finished last.
d. the numbers on a lottery ticket.
e. the color of shoes people wear to school.

14. The cases in a random sample are chosen (55)
a. in such a way that each case has an equal chance of being selected.
b. haphazardly.
c. in the easiest way possible.
d. by their relative ranks on one of the variables of interest to the research.
e. by having a third party make the selection.

15. Anthropologists use tests of statistical significance (56)
a. to prove their hypotheses.
b. to prove their theories.
c. to demonstrate the theoretical importance of their work.
d. to determine whether their results can be attributed to chance.
e. in order to guarantee that their samples are indeed random.

16. When a researcher finds a statistically significant relationship, the *least* likely problem with the study is that (56-57)
a. the researcher used a biased sample.
b. the result is due to chance.
c. the researcher ignored many important variables.
d. the theory behind the study contains logical inconsistencies.
e. the measures adopted by the researcher are inadequate.

17. Exceptions to predicted relationships in a cross-cultural study are *least* likely to be due to (57)
a. the presence of other causes for the phenomenon.
b. cultural lag.
c. people's desire to affirm their individuality.
d. measurement inaccuracy.
e. the possibility that a theory is wrong.

18. One advantage a non-historical controlled comparison has over a cross-cultural study is that (58)
a. in a controlled comparison the anthropologist can have greater knowledge of the region under study.

b. a controlled comparison allows an anthropologist to test hypotheses as well as formulate theories, while a cross-cultural study does not.
c. a controlled comparison is less expensive than a cross-cultural study.
d. a controlled comparison allows the anthropologist to generalize research findings to a larger sample of societies.
e. the controlled comparison provides more reliable results.

19. The cross-cultural method is limited in that (58-59)
a. anthropologists cannot *test* explanations with this method.
b. anthropologists are dependent on information that already appears in available ethnographies.
c. anthropologists who use this method often become mired in the ethnographic details of particular societies and find it difficult to make generalizations.
d. traits from different societies cannot be compared because they are always adjusted to the particular society.
e. it gives researchers only a limited view of the full-range of human cultures.

20. One advantage of historical research is that (59-60)
a. it allows for the easy testing of hypotheses.
b. it helps us determine if hypothesized causes of specific phenomena truly precede these phenomena in time.
c. it is based on reliable accounts of foreign cultures written mostly by trained anthropologists.
d. it helps us sort through the irrelevant facts to get to the main variable that really causes change.
e. we have good historical records covering hundreds of years for most of the societies anthropologists have studied.

Study Questions

1. What are the relationships between associations, statistical associations and a laws?

2. How are associations, hypotheses and theories related?

3. What do anthropologists mean when they say they make predictions based on their theories?

4. In what ways might theoretical orientations help in generating theories? What are the limitations?

5. Outline the procedure researchers follow to test theories. What are the roles of hypotheses, operational definitions, sampling and statistical evaluation?

6. What are some of the limitations of ethnohistory in the study of theory? To what extent can other techniques, like controlled comparison or cross-cultural research, surpass these limitations?

Answers to Review Questions

1)d; 2)b; 3)law; 4)theories; 5)a; 6)d; 7)b; 8)hypotheses; 9)b; 10)d; 11)d; 12)b; 13)d; 14)a; 15)d; 16)b; 17)c; 18)a; 19)b; 20)b

Chapter 5

Language and Culture

Chapter Outline

I. Communication
  A. Animal communication
  B. The origins of language

II. Structural linguistics
  A. Phonology
  B. Morphology
  C. Syntax

III. Historical linguistics
  A. Language families and culture history
  B. The processes of linguistic divergence

IV. Relationships between language and culture
  A. Cultural influences on language
    1. Basic words for colors, plants and animals
    2. Focal areas
    3. Grammar
  B. Linguistic influences on culture: The Sapir-Whorf hypothesis

V. The ethnography of speaking
  A. Social status and speech
  B. Sex difference in speech

Overview

This chapter is about human language -- its origin, its structure, the ways it changes, and the relationships between culture and language.

Linguists have identified between 4000 and 5000 mutually unintelligible human languages, some 2000 of which are still spoken today. Human languages grew out of the communication systems common to other animals. Non-humans communicate through smells, sounds, and body movements. Other animals, including vervet monkeys, have symbolic language -- in the sense of using learned symbols to refer to things that are absent. But humans use many more symbols than other animals, and are able to combine different utterances to produce an infinite number of phrases with new meanings. That is, human languages are *open*. Although chimpanzees and gorillas have been taught to use open languages, they have never been observed using an open language in the wild. Study of the languages of "primitive" cultures cannot tell us much about the origin of human speaking since no contemporary language is any more primitive than any other. However, some linguists think we can learn something about the universal biological basis of language by observing how children learn to speak and by studying the development of new Creole languages. Children the world over learn to speak at about the same age. By 12 or 13 months they can name a few objects and actions, and by 18 months they can combine two words to make a sentence. Similarly, Creole languages everywhere have strikingly similar grammars, including the use of a change in pitch in the voice to transform a declarative sentence into a question, the use of particles to express the future and past tenses, and the use of a double negative. These are characteristics also found among children's speech.

To describe languages linguists must discover the rules that determine how sounds are to be made and combined to produce meaningful utterances. This requires identifying the phonemes, morphemes, morphology and syntax of a language. Phonemes are sets of varying sounds (phones) that do not change the meaning of a word. Morphs are the smallest units of meaning in a language. Several morphs may all mean the same thing (such as the various ways to form the plural in English) and thus make up a single morpheme. Morphology is the study of morphs. Syntax is the study of how the ordering of morphs affects meaning.

Historical linguists compare similar contemporary languages in order to reconstruct their common ancestor. They also use vocabulary items to determine the location of the homeland of the people who spoke the ancestral language. For example, common Indo-European words for certain trees found in the Eastern Ukraine suggest that this area was the homeland of the original proto-Indo-European speakers, an inference further backed up by archeological data. Linguists also assume that the place with the greatest diversity of dialects represents the homeland from which groups splintered off to colonize new areas. The languages spoken near the "home-base" of a language family should also show more similarities with neighboring language families, presumably, because they all derived from some even older language in the more distant past.

Historical linguists also study the processes of linguistic change and diversification. Research shows that both geographical and social boundaries can create different dialects. People tend to speak the way their friends speak, regardless of how much they must also talk to non-friends who speak a different dialect. Languages can also borrow from each other. Vocabularies are borrowed more easily than grammars or phonology.

Culture may influence language in several ways. The number of simple terms for colors, plants and animals increases with societal complexity. The simplest societies generally have basic color terms only for "dark" and "light." The next color term to be added is "red." Only afterwards do "yellow," "green," and "blue" enter the vocabulary. Although simpler societies can express other colors, they must do so by referring to objects in their environments (for example, "the color of a young pandanus leaf"). More complex societies also have more general terms for plants and animals (for example, "birds" as opposed to "robins"). It seems the general terms increase when ordinary people have less and less to do with specific plants and animals. The core (non-specialized) vocabularies of all languages appear to be roughly the same size, but different languages have more elaborate vocabularies for those items most important in the culture. Culture may also affect the grammar of a language. For example, the expression "to have" is generally found only in the languages of stratified societies with private property.

Anthropologists disagree as to whether language can affect other aspects of culture. Some suggest that language perpetuates stereotypes of male dominance. One study comparing Hebrew, English and Finnish speaking children showed that children tend to recognize themselves as either boys or girls earliest where the language most emphasizes gender (Hebrew), and latest where it does not (Finnish).

Sociolinguists study the ways language is used in different contexts. For example, in English people address people differently (first name, last name or title) according to the formality of the situation and the status of the people involved. Among the Nuer different forms of address are used when talking to people of different age and kin categories. In many societies males and females have different ways of speaking. In English women use pronunciation and grammatical forms that are closer to standard English (the English heard on radio and television) than do men.

Common Misunderstandings

Many people feel that some languages and dialects are more "correct" or "pure" than others. Yet there is no absolute or "scientific" criterion for establishing what the proper way of speaking should be. Since languages are constantly changing, and constantly borrowing vocabulary from other tongues, there has never been a "pure" form of any language. In strictly linguistic terms Puerto Rican Spanish is just as correct as Castillian Spanish, Québecois just as good as Parisian French, and American Black dialects just as "pure" as Oxford English. If some ways of speaking are considered more "correct" than others, this is mostly because cultural norms dictate the "proper" way of speaking in different contexts. It may be comforting to realize that Oxford English would be considered just as clumsy in Harlem as would Black dialects in upper crust British society.

Key Terms and Concepts

ASL	morph
bound morpheme	morpheme
closed communication system	morphology
cognates	open communication system
core vocabulary	phone
creole languages	phoneme
descriptive linguistics	phonology
dialects	pidgin languages
ethnolinguistics	protolanguage
free morpheme	sibling language
grammar	sociolinguistics
historical linguistics	structural linguistics
language family	symbolic
lexical content	syntax

Review Questions

1. By "symbolic" communication, anthropologists mean that (64)
a. religious elements are included.
b. the communication is learned and has meaning even if the thing referred to is not present.

c. visual signs are involved.
d. meaning is unnecessary, the primary objective being the communication of feeling.
e. the communication does not involve feeling.

2. In contrast to humans, no animals have been observed in the wild to use (64-65)
a. a vocal form of communication.
b. a symbolic means of communication.
c. a closed system of communication.
d. an open system of communication.
e. a communication system that involves meaning as opposed to feeling.

3. Humans have succeeded in teaching chimpanzees and gorillas all of the following *except* (65-67)
a. to invent new words when presented with new objects
b. communication via symbols
c. hundreds of vocabulary items
d. the combining of different words to form new meaning
e. to habitually use open communication systems in the wild.

4. Most anthropologists feel that human languages probably developed (67)
a. from call systems in which more than one call could be combined to produce a new meaning.
b. out of sign languages used by Neandertals who did not have the throat and mouth anatomy to permit speech.
c. when open call systems were divorced from their instinctual origins and became symbolic.
d. all at once with the emergence of Homo habilis and a much more complex brain.
e. more than 5 million years ago, as dated by historical linguists.

5. Compared to the languages spoken by technologically advanced, literate peoples, the languages spoken by primitive peoples in the world today (67)
a. are equally complex, with the average person using roughly the same sized vocabulary.
b. are simpler in terms of grammar and syntax.
c. are more complex, with greater vocabularies.
d. have far smaller core vocabularies.
e. generally have more general terms for colors and life-forms.

6. The human capacity for language is thought to be (67-68)
a. a shared cultural trait.
b. an acquired characteristic.
c. learned during the first few weeks of infancy.
d. an inborn genetic characteristic.
e. greater in some societies than in others.

7. Compared to children in complex societies, children in simpler societies (68)
a. learn different language skills at a somewhat later age.
b. learn different language skills at the same age.
c. sometimes learn language skills in a slightly different order -- for example vocabulary may develop much farther before words are combined.

d. learn different language skills at a somewhat earlier age.

e. are more likely to learn language skills from their mothers rather than their peers.

8. Creole languages (69)

a. are incomplete simplified languages.

b. are amazingly different in different parts of the world.

c. have grammars derived almost entirely from their master's language.

d. are amazingly similar in their grammars all over the world.

e. usually have no way of asking a question.

9. In contrast to the grammar taught in school, grammars written by linguists (69-70)

a. are more professional in describing the "correct" way of speaking.

b. consist of the often unconscious principles that predict how most people talk.

c. are not based on "rules" but on anarchy.

d. are designed to show people how they *ought* to speak whether they actually speak this way or not.

e. do not distinguish between different parts of speech like nouns and modifiers.

10. If the sounds {l} and {r} can be used interchangeably at the beginning of words in a given language without changing the meanings, then we say that (70)

a. these sounds are different phones of the same phoneme.

b. these sounds constitute different phonemes.

c. the language is deficient in phonemes.

d. these sounds are part of the same phone.

e. this is an agglutinating language.

11. One or more morphs with the same meaning make up a(n) (71)

a. morphology.

b. phoneme.

c. syntax.

d. morpheme.

e. endomorph.

Match the term with the description that fits it best.

a. the smallest unit of language that has meaning

b. the rules that predict how phrases and sentences are generally formed

c. study of what words are and how they are formed

d. a set of varying sounds that do not make any difference in the meaning of an utterance.

e. an incomplete, simplified version of a dominant language used for communication among peoples speaking various diverse languages.

12. pidgin _____ (69)

13. phoneme _____ (70)

14. morphology_____ (71)

15. morph _____ (71)

16. syntax _____ (72)

17. Which of the following is an example of a bound morpheme? (72)
a. the "er" in "the man came closer."
b. the word "man" in "the man sat on the bench."
c. the exclamation point in "the man sang alleluia!"
d. the "c" in "the man clapped his hands."
e. the intonation of the voice in "the man saw you there?"

18. Which of the following would linguists *not* assume about the location of the people who spoke a protolanguage? (74)
a. The point of origin of a language is the place where there is the greatest diversity of dialects.
b. Those plant and animal words that are cognates across the most number of languages represent the plants that were common in the home of the people who spoke the protolanguage.
c. Those who have the most antiquated forms of speech are generally located in the area of the homeland.
d. The non-related languages spoken in or near the homeland should show more similarity than exists between non-related languages in colonized areas.
e. Colonized areas generally show fewer differences in dialect than the home area.

19. Studies of dialect diversity in northern India suggest that (77)
a. dialectical differences are easily maintained if there are no friendships and easy going communication between different people.
b. even limited contact between people because of work greatly reduces dialect differences.
c. mass communication has greatly reduced dialect diversity in the area.
d. most of this diversity is geographical, with very little variation between different castes.
e. dialect differences are unrelated to geography, having much more to do with caste position.

20. Languages generally have more basic color terms (78-79)
a. when there are more left-handed people who speak the language.
b. when they have a darker eye pigmentation.
c. when there are relatively more women in the society because women generally distinguish more colors.
d. when they are spoken by people in more complex cultures.
e. when they are spoken by people living near the equator because nature is more colorful there.

21. Support for the idea that culture affects the grammar of a society is the finding that (81)
a. the possessive transitive verb ("to have")   is generally absent in cultures lacking private property.
b. upper class people generally speak more correctly than do lower class people.
c. nomadic cultures generally emphasize spans of time (e.g. "hours") rather than specific moments (e.g. "noon") to mark time periods.

d. sentences are generally longer in societies with large bureaucracies, because long sentences are harder to understand. This makes it more difficult to blame people for poor decision-making.
e. more highly stratified cultures generally depart further from the "instinctual" grammatical features found in Creole languages and children's speech. This is because upper class people attempt more to differentiate themselves from their peers.

22. Some support for the idea that language may affect culture comes from (82)
a. studies of when children identify themselves as male or female in cultures with languages that emphasize or deemphasize gender in their words.
b. studies of how children learn about movement in cultures with and without verbs that stress motion.
c. studies showing that where languages do not have terms for time intervals, people are less accurate at determining when a minute is over.
d. studies demonstrating that societies with fewer color terms are less interested in color in their art and more interested in form.
e. studies showing that people perceive the differences between similar colors if they have words to describe the differences.

23. Studies of the speech habits of different classes in England show that (83)
a. upper class people vary more among themselves in the ways they speak.
b. lower class people vary more among themselves in the ways they speak.
c. the lower classes use upper class dialects when addressing the upper classes.
d. the upper classes generally adopt lower class speech patterns when addressing the lower classes.
e. there is very little difference in the vocabulary and grammatical structure of upper class and lower class dialects. The differences are overwhelmingly questions of accent.

Study Questions

1. How do animals communicate in the wild? What is the evidence that some of this communication may be symbolic?

2. How are the languages taught to chimpanzees and gorillas similar to human language? What are the differences?

3. What do the linguistic errors children make and the grammars found in all Creole languages have in common? How can these similarities be explained?

4. How can historical linguistics tell us about the culture of past societies? Give examples.

5. What cultural features are related to the number of basic color terms and general terms for plants and animals in a language? Why?

6. How might language affect other aspects of culture? What is the evidence?

7. What are some of the different ways Americans, Javanese and the Nuer talk when addressing different kinds of people? Why?

Answers to Review Questions

1)b; 2)d; 3)e; 4)a; 5)a; 6)d; 7)b; 8)d; 9)b; 10)a; 11)d; 12)e; 13)d; 14)c; 15)a; 16)b; 17)a; 18)c; 19)a; 20)d; 21)a; 22)a; 23)b

Food Getting

Chapter Outline

Overview

    This chapter deals with how people make their living. Anthropologists usually categorize societies into four different food-getting technologies: 1) food-collectors, 2) horticulturalists, 3) intensive agriculturalists, and 4) pastoralists. Before about 10,000 years ago all human beings lived by food-collecting. Today food-collectors (hunter-gatherers) are found mostly in marginal environments unsuitable for agriculture. For example, the Ngatatjara aborigines live in Australia's inhospitable Gibson desert. They lead a nomadic life in which women collect plant foods and men hunt animals like lizards, emus or kangaroos. The Copper Eskimo live in the Canadian Arctic. Their life is more seasonal than the aborigines'. In the winter the Copper Eskimo live near the shore and depend on seals and polar bears for food; in the spring and summer they move to inland lakes, where they fish and hunt caribou to stock up for the fall, when they spend their time preparing tools and clothing for winter. Most hunter-gatherers live in small communities, in sparsely populated territories. They generally lead nomadic lives, and have no individual land rights or social classes. Although called traditionally "hunter-gatherers" 38% of these societies actually get most of their food from fishing. Thirty percent get most from gathering and only 25% get most of their food from hunting. Studies of Australian Aborigines and of the !Kung suggest that these societies may enjoy a good deal of leisure time.

By horticulture, anthropologists mean the growing of crops in fields that are not permanently cultivated. The most common type of horticulture is *extensive* or *shifting* agriculture, in which land is cultivated for a few years and then left idle for a larger number of years. The Jívaro Indians who live on the eastern slopes of the Andes, and are famous for their head-shrinking practices, practice this kind of agriculture. Another kind of horticulture is based on permanent tree crops such as the breadfruit, coconut and banana trees cultivated by the Samoans. Horticultural societies generally support more people per unit land, and are generally more sedentary than hunter-gatherers. They often have some craft specialization.

Intensive agriculturalists cultivate fields on a permanent basis, using plows, irrigation, and fertilizers. In the rural Greek village of Vasilika men prune grape vines and hoe wheat fields, while women tend the cotton crops. The whole family helps during the harvest season, but specialists are called in to do things like repair roofs or gin cotton. In rural Vietnam farmers depend mostly on rice which is stored for family consumption, used to pay hired hands and sold on the market. Intensive agriculturalists usually work more hours than simpler agriculturalists. They are also more likely to suffer food shortages, perhaps because the greater reliance on only a few crops means people run a greater risk of failure from plant disease, or because planting for a market means people are subject to the vagaries of market prices. Commercialization of agriculture is resulting in greater mechanization, the use of hired labor rather than family labor, and a reduction in the proportion of the population engaged in agriculture.

Specialized pastoralists depend mostly on their herds of animals. Often, most of their animal protein comes from living animals in the form of milk and blood products. A large portion of their food energy comes from agricultural products obtained through trade. The Basseri of southern Iran live in a dry area and raise sheep, goats, camels and donkeys. They migrate regularly with their animals to the mountains in summer and to the lowlands in winter, living in tents made of woven goat hair. The route along which they pass is considered tribal "property." The Lapps in northwestern Scandinavia herd reindeer, either under an extensive system in which the animals wander over a large area, or under an intensive system in which they are fenced in. Pastoral communities are usually small. Individuals or families own their own animals and other personal possessions, but decisions about when and where to move are made by the community. Trade is very important.

The classification by James of the world's surface into eight different types might partly explain why people in different places have different food-getting techniques. 1) *Dry lands* constitute 18% of the world's land surface, but only 6% of its population. When technology is simple, hunting-gathering seems to be the major form of food-getting in dry lands. With irrigation, intensive agriculture is possible. Apparently, horticulture is not possible in such areas, although pastoralism may be. 2) *Tropical forest* lands make up 10% of the earth's surface and 28% of its population. The most common forms of food-getting in such areas are horticulture or rice paddy cultivation. 3) *Mediterranean scrub forests* make up 1% of the earth's surface and 5% of its population. They are excellent habitats for all forms of food-getting. 4) *Mixed forest* lands constitute 7% of the world's surface, but 42% of its population, are excellent for intensive agriculture and other food-getting techniques. 5) *Grasslands* make up 19% of the earth's surface and 10% of its population, supporting hunting and gathering, specialized pastoralism, and more recently, intensive agriculture. 6) *Boreal forests* occupy 10% of the earth, but only 1% of its population, and are unsuited for agriculture. 7) *Polar lands* occupy 16% of the earth and 1% of its population. The Eskimos living there subsist by hunting and fishing. 8) *Mountain lands* constitute 12% of the earth's surface and 7% of its population. Today these areas are occupied by pastoralists and intensive agriculturalists. In addition to the associations of food-getting technologies with these land types, anthropologists have also discovered that approximately 80% of the world's horticultural societies are found in the tropics, while 75% of societies with intensive agriculture are not found there.

Since hunting and gathering is usually more secure and requires less work than agriculture, most anthropologists feel that hunters and gatherers adopted agriculture because they were forced to do so. The main pressure to cultivate may have come from: a) population pressure in an area of abundant wild food sources, b) population growth which "filled up" the world, or c) the emergence of greater seasonal variation in rainfall. Similarly, intensification of agricultural production may also be due population growth.

Common Misunderstandings

Some people feel that the failure of a society to practice agriculture is a result of ignorance. However, as the text makes clear, a hunting and gathering way of life may be more comfortable than an agriculture one. Hunter-gatherers appear to enjoy more leisure time, better diets, better health, and less risk of food shortages than do agriculturalists. Likewise, horticulturalists may be better off than intensive agriculturalists. Hunters-and-gatherers have managed to continue up to the present day in some areas of the world primarily because their marginal environments, and lack of population pressure have made intensive agriculture less attractive here than elsewhere.

Key Terms and Concepts

agribusiness
boreal lands

cash crops
commercialization

extensive cultivation
food collection
food production
grasslands
horticulture
igloos
il-rah
intensive agriculture
marginal areas
maupok seal hunting
"mediterranean" scrub forest
mixed forest

oases
pastoralism
polar lands
prairies
rice paddy agriculture
savannas
shifting cultivation
slash-and-burn agriculture
social differentiation
steppes
subsistence technology
tundras

Review Questions

1. The term "subsistence technology" refers to a society's (89)
a. implements used to gather food.
b. means of obtaining food.
c. agricultural tools.
d. arsenal for defense against animals and other humans.
e. most sophisticated tools.

2. A food-collecting society would not obtain food by (89)
a. fishing
b. gathering wild plants.
c. hunting.
d. cultivating plants
e. trapping.

3. Today, hunters and gatherers are mostly found in (89)
a. marginal areas of the earth.
b. tropical rainforests.
c. deserts.
d. mountainous regions.
e. remote regions of the Amazon.

4. One of the differences between contemporary hunter-gatherers and prehistoric hunter-gatherers is that (91)
a. prehistoric hunter-gatherers depended more on fishing, while contemporary hunter-gatherers depend more on hunting.
b. prehistoric hunter gatherers were not restricted to marginal areas.
c. contemporary hunter-gatherers are generally exposed to fewer illnesses.
d. contemporary hunter-gatherers sometimes gain their foods from cultivation.
e. contemporary hunter-gatherers are healthier.

5. Compared to other subsistence strategies, hunting and gathering usually implies (93)
a. greater risk of famine.
b. longer work hours.
c. more male dominance.
d. higher reproductive rates.
e. more nomadism.

6. Surveys of different food-collecting societies around the world show that which of the following foods is generally most important? (93)
a. hunted animals.
b. gathered fruits and tubers.
c. fish.
d. gathered insects and reptiles.
e. cultivated foods obtained through trade.

7. In anthropology horticulture refers to (93)
a. the growing of vegetables in small gardens, generally with the use of fertilizers.
b. the growing of flowers for sale.
c. the use of irrigation to cultivate crops on a permanent basis.
d. the use of simple tools and long periods of fallow.
e. the growing of food crops in small permanent gardens.

8. The two major kinds of horticulture distinguished by anthropologists are (93)
a. dependence on tree crops and paddy rice.
b. shifting cultivation and intensive agriculture.
c. plow agriculture and irrigation agriculture.
d. shifting cultivation and dependence on tree crops.
e. extensive agriculture and intensive agriculture.

9. Which of the following crops requires the least work? (94-95)
a. cotton in rural Greece.
b. rice in Vietnam.
c. manioc among the Jívaro.
d. grapes in rural Greece.
e. breadfruit among the Samoans.

10. Which of the following is *not* generally a consequence of the shift from food-collecting to horticulture? (95)
a. more food obtained from a smaller area.
b. more sedentary populations.
c. more leisure time.
d. more social differentiation.
e. less nomadic lifestyle.

11. Intensive agriculture refers to (95)
a. the use of long fallow periods to replenish the soil's fertility.
b. the use of a large area of land to support a family with cultivated foods.
c. the growing of crops for sale.
d. the use of different techniques to cultivate fields continuously.
e. the planting of crops for family consumption only.

12. Food shortages are most likely to occur in which type of society? (98)
a. slash-and-burn agriculturalists
b. food-collectors
c. societies dependent on tree-crops
d. fishing societies
e. intensive agriculturalists

13. In societies with intensive agriculture (98)
a. people generally work more than among horticulturalists.
b. people generally work fewer hours per day than among horticulturalists.
c. men generally work more than women.
d. women generally work less on food processing and chores around the home.
e. people enjoy more security against famine.

14. Which of the following is generally *not* associated with the increased commercialization of agriculture (98)
a. less risk of food shortages
b. more mechanized technology
c. proportionally fewer people practice agriculture
d. agribusinesses
e. increased dependence on buying and selling.

15. The diet of pastoral peoples (99)
a. consists in large part of agricultural food obtained through trade.
b. usually consists mostly of milk, blood and eggs.
c. is secure against food shortages.
d. is usually inadequate in complete proteins.
e. consists mostly of meat.

16. Which of the following does *not* generally characterize pastoral societies (101)
a. small communities of related families.
b. seasonal changes of residence.
c. communal ownership of grazing lands.
d. family ownership of animals
e. economic independence from surrounding agricultural societies.

Match the society with the description that fits it best.
a. call in specialists for tasks like repairing roofs or ginning cotton.
b. known for their practice of shrinking heads.
c. once described as "lazy" because their dependence on tree crops meant they did not need to work very much.
d. eat lizards hunted in the desert.
e. spend most of the time during the Fall preparing winter clothing and repairing or making tools.
f. paddy rice cultivation

17. Ngatatjara Australian Aborigines (91)
18. the Ecuadorian Jívaro (94)
19. Copper Eskimos (91-92)
20. Rural Greece (96-97)
21. the Samoans (94-95)
22. Rural Vietnam (97-98)

Match the physical habitat with the description that fits it best.
a. either hunting and gathering or intensive agriculture with irrigation practiced here.
b. supports 42% of the world's population.

4 0

c. located between mountains and the coast with mild rainy winters and hot dry summers.
d. most horticultural societies found here.
e. generally associated with either hunting and gathering or pastoralism, but large machines make intensive agriculture possible.

23. Tropical forest (102)
24. Dry lands (101-102)
25. Mixed forest lands (102)
26. grasslands (103)
27. "Mediterranean" scrub forest (102)

28. Today's anthropologists have suggested all of the following to explain the origin of agriculture *except* (104-106)
a. After the earth "filled up" with people, they were forced to get more food out of each area of land.
b. Excessive population growth in areas of abundant wild foods forced people to migrate into areas that had to be cultivated to produce well.
c. The discovery that agriculture is easier than hunting and gathering convinced many to turn to agriculture.
d. More seasonal variation in rainfall made agriculture necessary to get through the dry season.
e. The increasing difficulty of exploiting wild foods forced people to plant.

Study Questions

1. How are contemporary hunters and gatherers different from those living 100,000 years ago? Who lived better? Why?

2. How much do people work in societies with hunting-and-gathering, horticulture and intensive agriculture? What is the evidence? What does this imply about the origins of these different food-getting techniques?

3. Describe the ways food-collectors, pastoralists, and horticulturalists move about. What explains these settlement patterns?

4. How do food-collectors, pastoralists and horticulturalists differ in the kinds of things people can own? What explains these differences?

5. Describe physical habitats typical of food-collectors, pastoralists, horticulturalists and intensive agriculturalists. Why?

Answers to Review Questions

1)b; 2)d; 3)a; 4)b; 5)e; 6)c; 7)d; 8)d; 9)e; 10)c; 11)d; 12)e; 13)a; 14)a; 15)a; 16)e; 17)d; 18)b; 19)e; 20)a; 21)c; 22)f; 23)d; 24)a; 25)b; 26)e; 27)c; 28)c

Chapter 7

Economic Systems

Chapter Outline

I. The allocation of resources
    A. Natural resources: land
        1. Food collectors
        2. Horticulturalists
        3. Pastoralists
        4. Intensive agriculturalists
    B. Technology

II. The conversion of resources
    A. Incentives for labor
    B. Forced labor
    C. Division of labor
        1. By sex and age
        2. Beyond sex and age
    D. The organization of labor
    E. Decision-making about labor

III. The distribution of goods and services
    A. Reciprocity
        1. Generalized reciprocity
        2. Balanced reciprocity
            a. The Kula ring
            b. Other balanced systems
        3. Negative reciprocity
        4. Kinship distance and type of reciprocity
        5. Reciprocity as a leveling device
    B. Redistribution
    C. Market or commercial exchange
        1. Kinds of money
        2. Degrees of commercialization
        3. Why does money and market exchange develop?
        4. Possible leveling devices in commercial economies

Overview

This chapter attempts to explain why societies vary in their patterns of ownership, work and trade.

I. Ideas about ownership vary according to a group's food-getting techniques. 1) Food-collectors usually do not own land *individually*, but, especially when wild plant and animal resources are predictable and abundant, *groups* may claim exclusive access to their territories. Since they are usually nomadic, hunter-gatherers usually have few personal possessions, and while these may be the property of the person who made them, sharing is very common. 2)

Horticultural families cannot own land on a permanent basis, but once they have planted a garden or tree crops, the land is considered theirs to use until the garden is abandoned. Sometimes clans or other groups may claim exclusive access to their territories. Since horticulturalists are more sedentary, they may have more personal possessions than food-collectors, but borrowing is still very common. 3) Among pastoralists land, or the right to pass through someone else's territory, is generally owned by the community. However, animals and other possessions are family owned. Although they are nomadic, pastoralists have animals to carry their goods, and so may carry around more personal belongings than do food-collectors. 4) Intensive agriculturalists generally permit private ownership of land, although governments usually restrict the way the land can be used, and may confiscate the land for some specific purpose. Tools are usually private property, but may sometimes be purchased communally.

II. Societies vary in how much people work beyond what is necessary for survival. Where people produce food primarily for their own consumption (subsistence economies), there can be no "profit motive," so people generally work less than in commercial economies. Especially among food collectors, it would not make sense to try to produce more than one could consume. Extra effort would only exhaust the future food supply, and the surplus food would eventually rot. In most societies where people produce mostly for their own consumption, workers tend to put in more hours only when they have more dependents (like children or invalids) to support. However, in some subsistence economies people are motivated to produce more than they can consume in order to provide elaborate feasts for neighboring villages. The feasting between villages may serve as a regional "insurance policy" in areas where the risk of suffering a bad year is common. In more complex societies people may also be forced to work harder through taxation, corvée labor, tenant farming and slavery. In many societies people may be motivated to work harder in order to acquire prestige through giving things away.

In all societies people are assigned tasks based on their sex and age. Certain tasks like hunting large aquatic mammals or trapping and hunting game are almost always assigned to men. Other tasks like caring for children, cooking, cleaning, laundering and fetching firewood and water usually go to women. Children usually work more in food-producing economies, where parents also have larger workloads, and in some societies work groups are formally organized on the basis of age. With more complex technologies some people may also become part-time or full-time specialists. With simpler technologies work is usually organized on an informal family or kin basis. In more complex societies formal contracts become more important.

Anthropologists have also examined why people decide to devote their time to some work activities rather than others. Studies in food-collecting societies, like the Aché, show that people choose which animals to hunt based on how much meat **they** average for each hour of hunting. Food-producers also appear to choose how to devote their time based on the return they can get from different kinds of **work** even if they are not always aware of why they choose different jobs.

III. Goods may be distributed among different people according to the principles of reciprocity, redistribution or commercial exchange. There are three kinds of reciprocity. Generalized reciprocity refers to sharing -- the giving of gifts without expectation of immediate return. It is the form of exchange most common between individuals who know each other well in hunting-and-gathering and horticultural societies. Balanced reciprocity refers to trading with the expectation of immediate return. It is most common between *groups* in simple societies (for example, Trobrianders engage in *Kula* trading). In these cases trading partners are usually not closely related, but are of more or less equal status. Negative reciprocity refers to the attempt to take advantage of others, as in raiding one's enemies to steal cattle. Some anthropologists feel that reciprocal trading systems serve to equalize wealth across communities, as in the *potlatch* system of the northwest coast American Indians.

With redistribution people give goods to a chief who then gives them away again. In some societies, as among the Creek Indians, redistribution did not create differences in wealth, but in other societies, as among the Bunyoro of Western Uganda, the chiefs became wealthier than others by keeping some of the goods for themselves. One theory argues that redistribution developed in societies where chiefs were needed to coordinate exchanges between regions suitable for different kinds of crops. Another theory argues that redistribution served primarily as a way to stimulate people to produce more than they needed in order to offer feasts and store up "credit" in areas with the possibility of crop failures.

Monetary exchange seems to have developed in areas where food supplies regularly exceed the needs of the food-producers and where craft specialists need the foods others have to offer. Societies differ in their degree of commercialization. In some places, as in parts of Melanesia, people use only special-purpose money. Elsewhere, as in our own society, people use general-purpose money. Peasants are people who produce their own food, but also depend on sales of agricultural products. Some anthropologists have argued that customs, like the *fiesta* complex in highland Latin America or graduated income taxes, serve to level differences in wealth in commercial societies, but others point out that these customs fail to redistribute the most important productive resources like land, and have not resulted in greater equality.

Market exchange is most common in societies with higher levels of economic productivity. Market exchange of goods appears first, followed by market exchange of labor or credit, and finally market exchange of land, which appears only in societies at the highest levels of productivity.

Common Misunderstandings

Introductory economics textbooks often suffer from one common misunderstanding about primitive economic systems -- the idea that exchange began with barter between individuals. Sometimes these texts attempt to argue that money would have been a more efficient way of exchange for these primitive peoples. As we now know from anthropology, this idea is wrong. The most common form of exchange between individuals in most primitive societies is generalized reciprocity -- gift giving. Barter may occur, but only between groups or individuals who do not know each other well. The exchange system of simpler cultures may be perfectly adequate to their way of life, and may even have some advantages (like promoting equality) over our own money economies.

Key Terms and Concepts

balanced reciprocity
Chayanov's rule
corvée
fiesta complex
generalized reciprocity
general purpose money
Homestead act
Kula ring
leveling device
market society

monetary (commercial) exchange
negative reciprocity
optimal foraging theory
peasant economies
potlatch
production
redistribution
special purpose money
subsistence economy

Review Questions

1. The economic systems of different societies (110)
a. do not always specify who has access to resources.
b. are all based on either money or barter.
c. always include customs for distributing or exchanging goods and services.
d. refer only to the exchange systems found in the societies.
e. are also characterized by barter between individuals.

2. Individual ownership of land is most common among (113)
a. horticulturalists.
b. food collectors.
c. shifting agriculturalists.
d. intensive agriculturalists.
e. pastoralists.

3. Which of the following is most likely to be owned by an individual in a food-collecting society? (111,115)
a. water supplies
b. land
c. tools made by the individual
d. trees and other permanent sources of wild food
e. slaves

4. Anthropologists think food collectors are most likely to defend a group territory (111)
a. when resources there are scarce.
b. when the population is especially high.
c. when the population is small.
d. when resources there are abundant and predictable.
e. when resources are abundant, but unpredictable and the population relatively large.

5. Which of the following best characterizes horticultural societies? (112)
a. Individuals or families enjoy exclusive rights to use the gardens they have planted, but not to keep the land on a permanent basis.
b. Individuals or families own specific plots of land on which to make their gardens.

4 5

c. Land is generally not owned by any individual or group -- not even when it is being used.
d. Kin groups do not claim ownership to land.
e. Individuals do not own personal possessions.

6. Grazing lands among pastoralists are usually (112-113)
a. highly productive lands that could be used for agriculture.
b. owned by individual families.
c. located within a day's walk from people's farming territories.
d. owned communally.
e. traded between individual pastoralists during different periods of the year.

7. Animals among pastoralists are usually (112-113)
a. consumed by the people who raise them.
b. owned by individual families.
c. fed grains grown on the pastoralist's agricultural land.
d. owned communally.
e. used for the meat they provide the pastoralist's family.

8. An individual is most likely to own permanently a piece of land when (112-113)
a. there is enough land for all to have some property.
b. land is cultivated on a continuous basis.
c. individuals are unlikely to lose their land.
d. limited means of transportation force people to remain in the same place.
e. land is relatively unproductive.

9. One possible reason why people in subsistence economies work less than those in commercial economies is that (117)
a. in subsistence economies people are more likely to accumulate wealth, and use this wealth to "buy" leisure time.
b. people with subsistence economies have fewer children to support than do those in money economies.
c. in subsistence economies people earn nothing by working more since there is no market nearby to absorb the extra goods produced.
d. people with subsistence economies are generally too ill to work hard.
e. People in commercial societies usually work less than those with subsistence economies.

10. Data on Russian and Swiss peasants show that (117-118)
a. work inputs are determined primarily by individual personalities.
b. in families with proportionately more dependents, able-bodied workers generally work no harder than others.
c. Swiss peasants generally work harder than their Russian counterparts, primarily because capitalism provides greater incentives to work.
d. workers in families with more dependents generally work harder than others.
e. peasants generally work very little.

Match the term with the description that fits it best.
a. a form of direct forced labor for a limited period of time.
b. a monetary form of indirect forced labor.
c. the most extreme form of forced labor, in which individuals have little control over their labor.

d. a form of forced labor in which food producers must give part of their harvest to the owner of the land they work.

11. corvée_____ (119)
12. taxation_____ (118)
13. slavery _____ (120)
14. tenant farming_____(119)

15. Which of the following tasks is almost *exclusively* assigned to men in a society? (120)
a. collecting honey.
b. preparing soil for planting
c. making handicrafts out of stone.
d. weaving.
e. building houses.

16. Which of the following tasks is most likely to be assigned to women in a society? (120)
a. building houses.
b. making pottery.
c. collecting honey.
d. making nets.
e. fishing.

17. In which type of society do children generally work the most? (120-121)
a. society where women have more time to observe their children
b. food-collecting society
c. society where women work a great deal
d. society where heavy unemployment forces jobless parents to send their children to work.
e. society with low birth rates

18. Generalized reciprocity appears to increase (125)
a. during mild shortages of food.
b. during severe shortages of food.
c. when people who do not know each other well join together for a short period of time.
d. when food is especially abundant.
e. as people lose contact with their families of origin.

19. The *Kula* ring of the Trobriand Islanders is (126)
a. a puberty rite.
b. a ceremonial exchange of valued shell ornaments.
c. used in certain religious rituals.
d. a special piece of jewelry denoting social rank and wealth.
e. a dance formation used to determine who will have access to which area of land for gardening that year.

Match the type of exchange with the kind of relationship for which it is most frequently used.
a. exchange between strangers and enemies.
b. exchange among family members and close kin.

4 7

c. exchange involving the chief of a village.
d. exchange between equals who are not closely related.

20. balanced reciprocity _____ (125-127)
21. redistribution_____(129-131)
22. generalized reciprocity _____(124-125)
23. negative reciprocity_____(128)

24. Which of the following probably did *not* serve to equalize wealth between communities? (128-129,134)
a. the Pomo trade feasts
b. the potlatch of the Northwest coast Indians
c. the *fiestas* of highland Latin American communities
d. Melanesian pig feasts
e. the generalized reciprocity of the !Kung food-collectors

25. The difference between "special-purpose" and "general-purpose" money is that "special-purpose" money (131-132)
a. is issued only in emergency situations, such as high inflation periods.
b. is generally minted with special government insignia.
c. is used only for limited periods of time when cash is in short supply.
d. can be used only in limited kinds of exchange.
e. is designed primarily to smooth out the fluctuations in different currency exchange rates over time.

26. Which type of market exchange generally appears first in a society's history? (134)
a. market exchange of labor
b. market exchange of land
c. market exchange of goods
d. market exchange of credit
e. banking industries

Study Questions

1. What are the relationships between a society's food-getting strategy and its notions of personal or group property? Give examples.

2. What are some of the different forms of reciprocity used by people living in "primitive" societies? What accounts for these different forms?

3. Why in some societies are people encouraged to produce a surplus of goods, while in other societies this pressure does not exist? Include a discussion of food-collection, redistribution, "the profit motive" and taxation in your answer.

Answers to Review Questions

1)c; 2)d; 3)c; 4)d; 5)a; 6)d; 7)b; 8)b; 9)c; 10)d; 11)a; 12)b; 13)c; 14)d; 15)c; 16)b; 17)c; 18)a; 19)b; 20)d; 21)c; 22)b; 23)a; 24)c; 25)d; 26)c

Chapter 8

Social Stratification

Chapter Outline

I. Variation in degree of social inequality
   A. Egalitarian societies
   B. Rank societies
   C. Class societies
      1. Open class systems
      2. Caste systems
      3. Slavery

II. The emergence of stratification

Overview

This chapter deals with social inequality. While sociologists see all societies as stratified because they emphasize individual differences in status, anthropologists argue that some societies are egalitarian in the sense that they grant all families or other social groups equal access to status and privilege.

Egalitarian societies are common among most hunters and gatherers, and among some horticulturalists and pastoralists. Except for differences in age and sex, egalitarian societies grant positions of prestige to as many people as are capable of filling them. Prestige gained in one area is neither transferable to another area nor inheritable, and differences in prestige do not lead to differences in power or wealth. The Mbuti Pygmies of Zaire are one of the world's most egalitarian societies. In ranked societies some social groups have privileged access to prestige, but not to wealth or power. The Swazi of South Africa are an example. Class societies have unequal access to wealth and power, as well as to prestige.

In open class systems, as in the United States, it is possible for people to move from one class to another, although the vast majority of people remain in the class into which they were born. There are several reasons for this. First, wealth is often inherited. For example, in the United States most of the wealth of the richest people in the country was inherited from their parents. Also, criminal and other property laws in such societies usually favor the upper classes. Different access to education may also affect one's chances of rising or falling in the class system. In caste systems one's position in society is completely determined at birth. In India castes are associated with particular occupations and laws prohibit the mixing of classes, just as occurred in the United States during the segregation years, in Japan with the Eta people, and in Rwanda with the Tutsi, Hutu and Twa. Caste systems are most common in societies with intensive agriculture and a relatively undeveloped use of money, perhaps because the segregation of peoples is so closely associated with occupational obligations between peoples. With slavery, some people do not own their own labor. Systems of slavery have varied greatly in different societies. In ancient

Greece slaves normally came from conquered peoples. Among the Nupe of Nigeria they were either conquered in war or else purchased, but could eventually acquire their freedom.

Anthropologists are fairly certain that stratification developed only within the last 10,000 years, in conjunction with the intensification of agriculture and herding, the turn to a more settled lifestyle, political complexity and the presence of full-time specialization. Some scholars have suggested that stratified societies evolved out of rank societies, but there is no good empirical evidence to support this view. Others suggest that stratification may be decreasing. More highly industrialized countries generally show greater internal equality than do developing countries. This has led some scholars to conclude that the emphasis on professionals (who are valued for what they have learned) in technical societies leads to greater equality in access to wealth.

Common Misunderstandings

We are accustomed to living in a society with great inequalities, that professes to provide equal opportunities to all. Although economic differences are great, our government (but not business) leaders are elected. This is perhaps why we have so much trouble understanding how ranked societies could be so radically different. As the text points out, in some cultures prestigious families may be treated with all the deference accorded royalty in modern societies, and yet still be no wealthier than others. Leaders may inherit their positions, even though they must continue doing all the same chores done by everyone else. Part of the problem may be our confusion about what constitutes inequality. Obviously there is more than one kind of equality and a society may have great inequality of one type (e.g. wealth) but not others (prestige, power).

Key Terms and Concepts

age-set
caste
chiefdom
class society
closed class
egalitarian society

manumission
open class
rank society
slavery
stratification

Review Questions

1. According to anthropologists (138)
a. some societies are egalitarian.
b. all societies are stratified.
c. sociologists are wrong in assuming that all societies are stratified.
d. societies have been growing more and more egalitarian ever since agriculture first developed some 10,000 years ago.
e. all societies can easily be classified as "egalitarian," "ranked" or "stratified."

2. In what types of society are economic resources equally available to all members of a given age and sex category? (139-140)
a. ranked and "open class"

b. egalitarian and ranked
c. caste and ranked
d. stratified and egalitarian
e. stratified and ranked

3. Ranked societies generally have equal access to (140-141)
a. power, but not to prestige and wealth.
b. prestige, but not to wealth or power.
c. power and prestige, but not to wealth.
d. wealth and power, but not to prestige.
e. wealth, but not to prestige or power.

4. In a given society, if the number of prestigious positions for a given age or sex is adjusted to fit the number of candidates, this society would be described as _____. (139)

5. Which society is the most egalitarian? (140)
a. the Mbuti pygmies of central Africa
b. the Swazi of South Africa
c. Northwest coast American Indians
d. the United States
e. !Kung Bushmen

6. Which of the following is *least* likely to characterize the chief in a ranked society? (140-141)
a. receipt of deferential treatment by others
b. inheritance of the chiefly position
c. greater wealth than others in the society
d. living accommodations equal to those of others in the society
e. task of redistributing wealth

Match the society with the description that best fits it.
a. headman is merely a unifying symbol with no advantages or decision-making power.
b. no leaders
c. chief owns more cows than others, and organizes work parties
d. commoners must show deference by remaining lower than their leader at all times, even if this means they must crawl.
e. food-collecting society with ranking.

7. Trobriand Islanders _____(140)
8. !Kung Bushmen _____(140)
9. Mbuti pygmies _____(140)
10. Northwest Coast Indians _____ (141)
11. Swazi _____(140-141)

12. Unlike in ranked societies, in class societies (141)
a. some social groups have advantages in acquiring wealth.
b. some people have more prestige and status than others.
c. people generally do not need to show deference to those of higher status.

d. people have a greater chance to rise in the system.
e. lower-ranked people can more easily acquire prestige and status

13. Contemporary American society can be best classified as an example of (143)
a. an open class society.
b. a rigid caste society.
c. an egalitarian society.
d. a ranked society.
e. a redistributing society.

14. Studies in the United States show that (142)
a. prestige is generally unrelated to wealth in this country.
b. people tend to lump together the classes socially farthest from themselves, but make greater distinctions about class differences among those nearest to themselves in class.
c. people in this country have more equal access to positions of prestige and status than do people in most of the societies studied by anthropologists.
d. this country is basically egalitarian.
e. most of the wealth of the richest people comes from luck in the stock market.

15. In the United States (143)
a. the richest people inherit a greater percentage of their wealth than do poorer people.
b. people of all classes inherit roughly the same proportion of their wealth.
c. rich married women inherit most of their wealth from their husbands.
d. rich married women generally inherit a smaller proportion of their wealth than do rich married men.
e. the very wealthy manage to pass along their privileged status to their offspring primarily through providing a better education.

16. The top 2% of the United States population obtained most of their wealth from (143)
a. their shrewd stock investments.
b. high salaries in liberal professions.
c. inheritance from their parents.
d. entrepreneurial activities.
e. the application of high salaries in risky but highly profitable investments.

17. A society in which marriage between the classes is prohibited by law or custom is called (144)
a. a ranked society.
b. a caste society.
c. an egalitarian society.
d. an open class society.
e. a classless society.

18. One element generally *not* found in caste systems is (144-145)
a. the association of one's social position with one's occupation.
b. inheritance of one's status.

c. equal access to wealth.
d. differences in rank between individuals.
e. prohibitions on marrying those outside one's class.

19. Which of the following is *not* an example of a separate caste? (145-146)
a. Blacks in the segregated American South.
b. the Eta of Japan.
c. the Hutu of Rwanda.
d. the Brahmins of India.
e. the chiefly family among the Trobrianders.

20. Almost all forms of slavery systems provided some form of *manumission*. This most nearly means (145)
a. the sale of slaves.
b. inheritance of slaves.
c. the freeing of slaves.
d. rules regarding the marriage of slaves.
e. the capture of slaves.

21. Caste systems are most common in societies (148)
a. that were previously ranked.
b. with a tradition of slavery.
c. with a great deal of occupational specialization.
d. that have weak monetary systems, and intensive agriculture.
e. with personalistic political systems.

22. The idea that inequality may now be decreasing is based on data showing that (148)
a. highly industrialized nations have less inequality than primitive societies dependent on hunting and gathering or on horticulture.
b. highly industrialized nations have less inequality than nations that are only somewhat industrialized.
c. peasant societies are generally less stratified than horticultural societies.
d. world-wide the differences between rich and poor countries have been shrinking.
e. the wealthy are increasingly giving away a greater proportion of their wealth to charities.

Study Questions

1. Why do anthropologists and sociologists disagree about whether "egalitarian" societies exist?

2. What kinds of inequality are present in the kinds of society labeled by anthropologists as "egalitarian?"

3. Describe the leadership positions of the !Kung, the Swazi and Americans. In what ways are these positions different? What can each type of leader own?

4. How do most rich Americans obtain their wealth? What does this say about the phrase "all men are created equal"?

5. Describe the caste systems of India and Rwanda. How are they similar to or different from the U.S. and Japanese class systems?

Answers to Review Questions

1)a; 2)b; 3)d; 4)egalitarian; 5)a; 6)c; 7)d; 8)a; 9)b; 10)e; 11)c; 12)a; 13)a; 14)b; 15)a; 16)c; 17)b; 18)c; 19)e; 20)c; 21)d; 22)b

Sex and Culture

Chapter Outline

I. Sex differences
   A. Physique and physiology
   B. Social roles
      1. Productive and domestic activities
      2. Relative contributions to subsistence
      3. Political leadership and warfare
      4. The relative status of women
   C. Personality
      1. Myths about differences in behavior

II. Sexuality
   A. Cultural regulation of sexuality: permissiveness versus restrictiveness
      1. Childhood sexuality
      2. Premarital sex
      3. Extramarital sex
      4. Sex within marriage
      5. Homosexuality
   B. Reasons for restrictiveness

Overview

   This chapter deals with the different ways societies handle male and female social and sexual behavior.

I. Physically, humans everywhere are sexually dimorphic. Males are taller and heavier, have more body weight in muscle, greater grip strength, larger hearts and lungs and greater aerobic work capacity. Women have wider pelvises, and more of their body weight in fat.

   Societies differ in the chores they assign men and women. Some tasks, like the hunting of large sea mammals or warfare are almost always assigned to men. Others, like child-care or cooking, are more likely to be given to women. One theory (the "strength" theory) argues that the division of labor between the sexes results from the greater strength of males. The "compatibility-with-child-care" argument suggests that women cannot do tasks that are too dangerous or that cannot be interrupted for child-care. Although both of these theories may account for many of the jobs men and women do, neither can account for why men usually do such tasks as making musical instruments, or working bone, horn and shell. The "economy-of-effort" theory, when combined with these other theories, may explain these other tasks. It suggests that it is advantageous to perform tasks located near each other, or that one understands most. Finally, the "expendibility" theory suggests that men may do the dangerous tasks because their deaths will not seriously affect the reproductive capacity of the group. The granting of special prestige to these tasks may be a way to guarantee that men will want to do them. The "strength" and "compatibility" theories cannot account for why women do very heavy tasks in some societies, or why women manage to find ways to handle their children when they must do chores (like hunting among the Agta) that appear incompatible with child-care.

In most societies both men and women contribute food to the family, but men typically contribute more. Still, there are societies, like the Tchambuli of New Guinea, where women are the primary bread-winners. The major question needing explanation is why women do more of the farming in some societies, while in others men do more. In horticultural societies women generally contribute more to subsistence than men, but among intensive agriculturalists men contribute more. This may be because women in societies with intensive agriculture generally must spend more time on domestic chores, like processing grains, and because women in such societies normally have more children to care for. Also, in many horticultural societies women may be stuck with the farming, because men are away on making war. Where women contribute more to subsistence girl babies are preferred over boys, babies are fed solid foods earlier (meaning the mother is freer from nursing responsibilities), and girls are taught to be more industrious.

Men everywhere dominate political life. This may be because men are the warriors, and judgments about warfare may be the most important decisions to be made. Men may also dominate politics because they are generally taller than women, or because they know more about the outside world since their tasks take them farther from home. Women may also have trouble engaging in politics if their child-care duties prevent them from socializing with others. Cross-cultural studies show that women participate less in politics where communities are organized around male kin, and women participate more where children are brought up with more affection, perhaps because this upbringing makes them value "female" characteristics more.

The "status" of women is not a single phenomenon. For example, societies that place more value on women's lives are not necessarily those that grant women more influence, or that allow women to inherit property, or that have female gods. Higher status for women in many areas of life is associated with kinship systems organized around women, and with less political complexity. Western colonialism appears to have reduced women's status in many areas of the world. Higher status for women is unrelated to the relative contribution to subsistence of males or females and to the importance of warfare in a society.

Systematic cross-cultural studies suggest that universally males may be more aggressive than females, perhaps in part for biological reasons, perhaps in part because socialization pressures or the kinds of tasks generally assigned boys encourage aggressiveness. Girls are usually more responsible, more nurturant and more likely to conform to adult wishes and commands. Boys are more likely to dominate over others to get their own way. They are also more likely to play in larger groups, and to maintain a greater distance between each other. Some personality traits -- dependency, passivity and sociability -- clearly do not universally differentiate boys from girls.

II. Some societies are more restrictive about heterosexual activities than are others, although most societies ease sexual restrictions somewhat in adolescence. The Hopi are permissive about childhood sexuality, while "East Bay" society is restrictive. The Trobrianders and the Ila encourage premarital sex, while the Tepoztlan Indians are highly restrictive. Extramarital sexual relations are fairly acceptable among the Toda and the Chukchee, and more restrictive elsewhere. Most societies are more acceptant of male extramarital affairs than of female extramarital affairs. Societies also differ in their ideas about different kinds of sex acts within marriage, such as sex in public, at night, during menstruation or after pregnancy, and after the deaths of community members. Homosexuality is encouraged in some societies like the Siwans or the Etoro, and discouraged in others like the Lepcha.

Societies that are restrictive about one aspect of heterosexual sex are generally also restrictive about other aspects, but attitudes toward homosexuality are unrelated to attitudes toward heterosexual sex (with the exception that homosexuality is more common in societies that prohibit extramarital heterosexual relationships). Psychological interpretations relating homosexuality to parent-child relationships do not consistently predict which societies have more homosexuality. More restrictive attitudes toward homosexuality are generally found in societies where people are encouraged to have more children. More restrictive attitudes toward heterosexuality are generally found in complex societies, perhaps to ensure that people do not marry "beneath" their class.

Common Misunderstandings

People often talk as if different cultures could be easily classified according to how "male-chauvinist" or "sexually uptight" they are. However, cross-cultural evidence shows that such classifications are risky. Depending on the criterion chosen, societies may be classified differently. For example, knowing whether a society has female gods tells us nothing about whether its women can hold political offices, or whether women inherit property. Knowing whether a society is restrictive about premarital heterosexual relations tells us nothing about its attitudes toward homosexuality. In comparing societies we need to specify exactly what we mean by such terms as "male-chauvinist" or "sexually uptight."

Key Terms and Concepts

aerobic work capacity
dependency
double standard
longhouses

nurturance
purdah
sexually dimorphic

Review Questions

1. In all known human societies the average male (152)
a. has a lower aerobic work capacity than the average female.
b. is taller than the average female.
c. fishes more than the average female.

d. contributes more to subsistence than the average female.
e. is more responsible than the average female.

2. Which of the following is *most* likely to be performed by males? (153)
a. fishing
b. trapping small animals
c. making leather handicrafts
d. building houses
e. clearing land

3. One of the reasons men take over certain "female" tasks (like weaving or cooking) when these products are commercialized is that (153-154)
a. women are less able to tolerate long periods of work than are men.
b. men are more likely to try to excel at these crafts, a characteristic important when articles are put up for sale.
c. men usually prefer to handle chores involving money.
d. performing a specialized craft for sale often involves uninterrupted work, which is incompatible with child-care.
e. Men do *not* usually take over these tasks.

4. Greater industrialization usually (157)
a. implies a stronger division of labor by sex because men are better able to support a family through their labor alone.
b. results in a breaking down of a strict sexual division of labor possibly because machines replace human strength and women can pay others to care for their children.
c. has implied a reduction in women's participation in the formal work force.
d. has no effect on the sexual division of labor.
e. creates a greater division of labor by sex because couples must move away from relatives who might otherwise have taken care of their children.

5. One reason women farm less than men in societies with intensive agriculture may be that (158-159)
a. intensive agriculture generally requires less work overall than does horticulture.
b. the grain crops grown by intensive agriculture typically require more processing time, forcing women to spend their time on household chores.
c. increased warfare makes it more dangerous for women to work on the fields in intensive agricultural systems.
d. women cannot handle the weeding that is often required in intensive agricultural systems.
e. people in these societies typically raise fewer children, and so do not need to produce so much food.

6. In societies where women contribute relatively more to subsistence (159)
a. there are more likely to be female gods.
b. women are more likely to enjoy formal leadership positions.
c. women generally enjoy higher status
d. girls are more likely to be taught to be industrious.
e. people are more likely to prefer sons over daughters.

7. Which of the following is *least* likely to explain why males almost universally dominate in politics? (159-161)
a. the fact that men are generally stronger than women, and that force is often needed to maintain leadership positions.
b. the fact that men are almost always the warriors and warfare is an important aspect of politics.
c. the fact that men are generally taller than women.
d. the fact that women generally must care for the children, which might make them less able to make the kinds of friends needed for politicking.
e. the fact that men generally travel farther afield and so know more about the things important to leadership.

8. Cross-cultural studies show that women are more likely participate in politics (161)
a. where they contribute more of the food than do the men.
b. where children are raised with greater affection and nurturance.
c. when the society is organized around male kin.
d. where both males and females are relatively taller.
e. where they bear more children.

Match the society with the description that best fits it .
a. women who care more for children have less influence than other women, possibly because they are less able to make friends.
b. women can go out of their house only with male approval, and then only covered from head to foot in a long black shroud.
c. matrilineal society where only men could hold political office, but where women could nominate, elect and impeach their male representatives.
d. women's hunting brings in almost 30% of the large game animals.
e. society where women contribute almost everything to subsistence through their fishing and trading activities.

9. Tchambuli of New Guinea _____ (157)
10. Daghara, Iraq _____ (161)
11. Agta of the Philippines _____ (156-157)
12. Iroquois Indians of New York State _____ (159)
13. Kayapo Indians of Brazil _____ (161)

14. Cross-cultural studies show that different types of women's status (162)
a. are not related to each other.
b. are closely related to each other.
c. generally coincide with the presence of female deities in the society's religion.
d. are all fairly closely related to the amount of food women contribute to subsistence.
e. are almost all higher in more complex societies.

15. Women are most likely to enjoy higher status in many different areas in (162)
a. societies where kin groups and marital residence are organized around women.
b. more complex societies.
c. societies where women contribute relatively more to subsistence.
d. societies with female deities.
e. societies with a great deal of warfare.

16. More often than not, Western colonialism has resulted in (163)
a. greater value given to women's farming abilities.
b. a decrease in women's rights to land.
c. a higher value placed on female deities, but a lower value placed on women's physical characteristics.
d. a lower value placed on women's lives, but greater political powers for women.
e. a higher value placed on women's work, but a lower value placed on her role as mother.

17. One of the problems with the argument that socialization for aggressiveness in boys is responsible for the universality of greater male aggressiveness is that (163-164)
a. there is no clear evidence that all societies socialize boys to be more aggressive.
b. males are not universally more aggressive.
c. studies in our society show that childhood socialization pressures have no effect on adult aggressiveness.
d. girls are sometimes socialized to be more aggressive than boys.
e. there is evidence of a gene for greater aggressiveness located on the Y chromosome.

18. Some researchers argue that the personalities of boys and girls are affected by the kinds of tasks they are assigned to do. This argument is supported by data showing that (165-166)
a. Navaho boys who stay at home are less aggressive than are Navaho girls who pasture sheep away from home.
b. Eskimo boys who go out hunting for seals are more aggressive than are Eskimo girls.
c. Luo boys who are forced to do female chores have more feminine personalities than other Luo boys.
d. Aché boys who refuse to go out hunting are more passive than are other boys.
e. societies where children do agricultural chores generally train children to be more openly aggressive than do societies where children mostly pasture animals.

19. The age when sexuality is least likely to be restricted is (167)
a. childhood.
b. infancy.
c. early married life.
d. adolescence.
e. old age.

Match the society with the description that fits it best.
a. sex at night is believed to cause blindness in the child conceived.
b. children are discouraged from touching their genitals in public, and boys older than five are taught to maintain their distance from girls.
c. visiting married men are permitted to have sex with their host's wife.
d. fathers arrange for other men to engage in sex with their unmarried sons.
e. homosexual sex thought better for society than heterosexual sex.
f. girls are given houses of their own where they can play at "being wife" with the boys of their choice.

20. Etoro of New Guinea _____ (170)
21. Chukchee of Siberia _____(169)
22. Chenchu of India _____ (169)
23. Siwans of Egypt _____ (170)
24. Ila of central Africa _____ (168)
25. "East Bay" Island in the Pacific _____ (168)

26. U.S. Studies carriend out in the 1940s and 1970s show that (167)
a. people have become much more lenient about extramarital sex.
b. the vast majority of Americans continued to reject extramarital sex.
c. more women than men have engaged in extramarital sex.
d. fewer than 10% of married American men have engaged in extramarital sex.
e. the frequency of premarital sex has remained about the same.

27. With regard to *when* married couples are allowed to have sex, Americans
    are (169)
a. unusually permissive.
b. unusually restrictive.
c. unusual in having neither formal nor informal restrictions of any kind.
d. about equally as restrictive as most other societies.
e. unusual in preferring the night rather than the daytime.

28. The societies that most restrict premarital sex (170)
a. generally are less restrictive about sex during childhood.
b. generally also restrict extramarital sex more.
c. generally are more tolerant of homosexuality.
d. generally are also less tolerant of homosexuality.
e. are less likely to emphasize modesty in dress.

29. Cross-cultural studies show that homosexuality is more acceptable in
    societies where (170-171)
a. warfare is more common.
b. capitalism flourishes.
c. people are less concerned about increasing their population.
d. warfare is less common.
e. the division of labor between men and women is greater.

Study Questions

1. What biological differences between human males and females appear to occur in all societies? How might these differences affect the kinds of tasks they do?

2. What are some of the problems with the "strength," "compatibility-with-childcare" and "male expendibility" theories regarding the sexual division of labor? How are these theories tied with the "economy-of-effort" theory?

3. How might we explain the tendency for women to contribute relatively less to subsistence than men in societies with intensive agriculture?

4. What are some of the cultural consequences of women's contributing more to subsistence? What is the evidence?

5. How might the universal lower participation of women in politics be explained? What might explain why women in some societies participate more than in others? What is the evidence?

6. What do anthropologists mean when they say that women's status is not a single phenomenon? What does this imply about our attempts to explain why women have higher or lower status in different societies?

7. Describe how attitudes toward sexual activities during marriage vary from one society to another. How might the differences be explained? Could these explanations account for American attitudes toward these practices?

8. Describe some of the ways societies differ in their attitudes toward homosexuality. How might these differences be explained? How well could these explanations account for recent changes in U.S. attitudes?

Answers to Review Questions

1)b; 2)b; 3)d; 4)c; 5)b; 6)d; 7)a; 8)b; 9)e; 10)b; 11)d; 12)c; 13)a; 14)a; 15)a; 16)b; 17)a; 18)c; 19)d; 20)e; 21)c; 22)a; 23)d; 24)f; 25)b; 26)b; 27)a; 28)b; 29)c

Chapter 10

Marriage and the Family

Chapter Outline

I. Marriage
  A. The Nayar "exception"
  B. Rare types of marriage
  C. Why is marriage universal?
    1. Division of labor by sex
    2. Prolonged infant dependency
    3. Sexual competition
    4. Other mammals and birds: postpartum requirements
  D. How does one marry?
    1. Marking the onset of marriage
    2. Economic aspects of marriage
        a. Bride price
        b. Bride service
        c. Exchange of females
        d. Gift exchange
        e. Dowry
  E. Restrictions on marriage: the universal incest taboo
    1. Childhood familiarity theory
    2. Freud's psychoanalytic theory
    3. Family disruption theory
    4. Cooperation theory
    5. Inbreeding theory
  F. Whom should one marry?
    1. Arranged marriages
    2. Exogamy and endogamy
    3. Cousin marriage
    4. Levirate and sororate
  G. How many does one marry?
    1. Monogamy
    2. Polygyny
    3. Polyandry

II. The family
  A. Variation in family form
    1. Extended family households
    2. Possible reasons for extended family households

Overview

This chapter begins a series of chapters on social organization. It first examines why marriage exists and why it takes different forms, and then looks at the different kinds of families that exist in different societies.

All societies have marriage, defined as a socially approved sexual and economic union between a man and a woman. The Nayar of India are exceptional in not having marriage, but since they are only part of a larger society, they do not contradict the assertion that all societies have marriage. A few societies allow marriages between members of the same sex. Among the Cheyenne Indians, married men sometimes took a *berdache* (male transvestite) as a second wife. and young Azande men from the Sudan customarily married boys by paying the boy's parents a brideprice. The Azande male-male marriages involved sexual relationships, but sexual ties may not have been a part of many female-female marriages. Many African societies allow marriages between women mostly in order to pass on kinship rights or to allow women to take on male roles.

Several theories have been proposed to explain why marriage is universal. According to one explanation, marriage is needed so that men and women can exchange the products of their labor. Another sees the long dependency period of infants as requiring cooperation between men and women in raising offspring. A third theory sees the constant receptivity of human females to sex as causing possibly harmful sexual competition unless marriage clearly defines sexual rights. The only theory supported by evidence from mammals and birds suggests that male-female bonding may exist to help raise offspring when females cannot simultaneously look for food and care for their young.

Societies mark the onset of marriage in different ways. The Trobrianders consider a couple married when they simply sleep together regularly. Other societies have elaborate ceremonies that include ritual expressions of hostility. Economic arrangements at marriage may include bride price, customary in 47% of the world's societies, bride service, female exchange, gift exchange and dowry. Bride price is most common where women work more than men and where men make most of the household decisions and may be a way to compensate the bride's relatives for the loss of a worker. Dowry is most common in monogamous, relatively complex, non-industrialized societies.

Anthropologists have discovered no society that permits ordinary people to engage in regular sexual relations with their mother, father, brothers or sisters. However, a few societies, like the ancient Egyptians, Incas and Hawaiians, did permit incest among royal families. One theory explains the near universality of the incest taboo by arguing that childhood-familiarity makes people uninterested sexually in each other as adults. This theory is supported by data from Israeli kibbutzim and from Taiwan showing that, despite cultural incentives to marry, people who had been brought up together were uninterested in each other sexually. In the United States studies show that fathers are more likely to have sexual relations with their daughters if they are absent during the daughter's first three years of life. While these data are consistent with the childhood familiarity argument, this theory fails to explain why people would need a *taboo* on incest if close relatives are already sexually uninterested in each other anyway. Sigmund Freud suggested that the taboo is a reaction against unconscious desires of children for their parents. Malinowski argued that the incest taboo prevents potentially dangerous sexual competition among family members. Both Freud's and Malinowski's theories fail to explain the need for a sexual taboo between siblings. The "cooperation" theory argues that the incest taboo helps guarantee people will marry outside their group, thus ensuring a wider range of kin to depend on in case of need. This theory does not explain why societies need a sexual taboo rather than simply a rule against marriage within the group. The inbreeding theory argues that the offspring of closely related parents are more likely to have harmful recessive genes. There is evidence from humans and animals to support this view.

Aside from the incest taboo, all societies also have other rules regulating marriage. In many cultures marriages are arranged by families or by go-betweens. In some places young people are encouraged to find their mates within their own kin group or community; others prefer them to marry outside this group. Most societies prohibit marriages between cousins, but some societies, such as those with dense populations where it is unlikely that cousins would marry each other anyway, do permit cousin marriages. Even some societies with sparse populations permit cousin marriages, probably because they have suffered recent depopulation which would greatly reduce the pool of potential mates. In many societies men are obliged to marry their brothers' widows, and women are obliged to marry their sister's widowers.

In most societies of the world some men are allowed to marry more than one woman (polygyny), and a few societies permit women to marry more than one man (polyandry). One theory explains polygyny as resulting from the need for men to have sexual outlets when their wives are under long post-partum sex taboos. A second theory suggests that polygyny provides the only means for all women to marry in societies where high male mortality in warfare has left fewer men than women. Noting that there are usually fewer older people than younger people in a society (especially where there are high fertility rates), a third theory suggests that a later age of marriage for males would result in polygyny, because this would leave fewer marriageable men than women. All of these theories receive statistical support, but when doing a statistical control analyses, only the sex-ratio theory and the late-age-of-marriage theory continue to predict which societies have polygyny. Polyandry may result from a skewed sex ratio in favor of males in a society.

Family living arrangements vary from one society to the next. A matrifocal family consists of a mother and her unmarried offspring. Nuclear families consist of a single couple and their unmarried offspring. Extended family households consist of two or more single-parent, monogamous, polygynous or polyandrous families linked by a blood tie, together with their offspring. More than half of the societies known to anthropology have extended family households. Extended families are most common where couples have "incompatible" activity requirements that prevent the mother from simultaneously caring for her children and doing other chores, or that prevent the father from carrying out his subsistence activities. In such cases the adult relatives in one's house can help baby-sit or do other chores when the parents are absent.

Common Misunderstandings

One common source of confusion for many people concerns testing explanations for things that are universal among humans -- like the incest taboo, or marriage. With no variation to play with, it is impossible to distinguish one theory about universals from another. In order to select one theory over another researchers must be able to make different predictions about which cases will have the trait in question and which will not. To distinguish different theories for human marriage the textbook had to report on cross-species studies. Although marriage may be universal among humans, it is not universal among animals; thus it was possible to predict which species had "marriage" (pair-bonding) and which did not. Another strategy would have been to look for cases that had less marriage than others -- for example, societies with a higher proportion of single people, or with higher divorce rates.

Key Terms and Concepts

berdache
bride price
bride service
cross cousin
dowry
endogamy
exogamy
extended family households
family of orientation
family of procreation
fraternal polyandry
genitor
group marriage
incest taboo

kibbutzim
kwashiorkor
levirate
marriage
matrifocal family
monogamy
nuclear family
parallel cousin
pater
polyandry
polygamy
polygyny
postpartum sex taboo
sororate

Review Questions

1. Which of the following is *not* part of the anthropological definition of marriage? (174)
   a. marriage is a social union
   b. marriage is a sexual union
   c. marriage is marked by a formal ceremony
   d. marriage is socially approved
   e. marriage is a bond between a man and a woman

2. The one group that did not have marriage is (174)
   a. the Winnebago Indians.
   b. the Trobrianders of New Guinea.
   c. the Nayar of India.
   d. the Masai of Kenya.
   e. the Mbuti pygmies of Zaire.

3. Among the Nayar which male was most responsible for helping a woman provide for her children? (175)
   a. her brother
   b. her husband
   c. her father-in-law
   d. her brother-in-law
   e. her lover

4. The Nayar do not contradict the statement that marriage is universal in human societies because (175)
a. Nayar couples cared for their children, even though these children were not their own.
b. recent research shows that a Nayar woman's lover actually carried out the role of husband, even if he was not called this.
c. the Nayar are not a complete society, but merely a caste within the larger Indian society.
d. the Nayar were a mythical society whose real existence has not been confirmed.
e. recent research shows that the Nayar's absence of marriage was simply a temporary phase in their history due to heavy warfare that kept the men away from their wives for long periods of time.

5. Among the Cheyenne Indians (175)
a. women sometimes married their brothers.
b. a man sometimes took a male transvestite as his second wife.
c. women sometimes married a boy before he was even born.
d. women were allowed to choose their husbands who were obliged to marry them.
e. men could only marry when they were well over 50 years old.

6. Among the Azande (176)
a. sexual relations between young men and boys often occurred even though the society strongly condemned these practices.
b. warriors sometimes married boys who performed female chores and had sex with them.
c. men were required to pay a higher brideprice for a boy-wife than for a female wife.
d. warriors captured boys from enemy groups and used them for sexual purposes.
e. some men, rather than marry women, preferred to marry boys.

7. Which of the following is most true? (175)
a. Marriages between two women were common in African societies where high male mortaliy in war meant that many women could not find male husbands.
b. Anthropologists have discovered no societies where women are permitted to "marry" other women.
c. In many societies women married other women to avoid having children.
d. In some African societies a female "husband" married another woman in order to enjoy the leadership roles only permitted to husbands.
e. Marriages between two women were common only in societies where high dowries meant that some women could not afford to marry a man.

8. The theory that women's constant receptivity to sex would create disruptive jealousies if it were not for marriage is problematic because (176)
a. in many animal species females are often receptive to sex, yet there is not much aggression over access to females.
b. there are many societies where jealousy simply does not exist.
c. those few societies that have no marriage show no signs of jealous conflict.
d. marriage is more likely the *cause* of jealousies, since unmarried people in most societies rarely exhibit jealousy.
e. women are more likely to be jealous of men's sexual exploits than vice-versa.

9. Which theory about human marriage is best supported by evidence from other species? (176-178)
a. the theory that a longer dependency period for infants requires that males help rear children.
b. the theory that a greater division of labor by sex encourages people to have readily available "trading partners."
c. the theory that pair-bonding results from the impossibility of a mother to simultaneously care for her offspring and search for food.
d. the theory that greater female receptivity to sex makes jealousy more problematic, thus encouraging males to claim specific females as theirs alone.
e. the theory that pair-bonding is primarily the result of religious teachings.

Match the society with the description that fits it best.
a. marriage is marked by the groom's public criticism of his bride's cooking.
b. marriage is marked by a mock fight between the bride and the groom.
c. go-betweens who negotiate with the bride's and groom's family to arrange the marriage spit on the bride's hands during the bridal ceremony.
d. marriage is marked by the exchange of insults between the bride's and groom's kin.
e. betrothal at puberty, and a trial period of living together

10. Taramiut Eskimo _____ (178)
11. Gusii of Kenya _____ (179)
12. Kwoma of New Guinea _____ (178)
13. Pukapukans of Polynesia _____ (179)
14. Reindeer Tungus of Siberia _____ (179)

15. Which form of economic exchange upon marriage is most common? (179-180)
a. bride price.
b. bride service.
c. gift exchange.
d. dowry.
e. exchange of females.

16. Compensation given to the bride's kin upon marriage is most common (180)
a. in societies where women work more than men.
b. in hunting and gathering societies.
c. in societies with intensive agriculture.
d. in societies with higher divorce rates.
e. in societies with matrilineages.

17. Dowry is most likely to be found in societies (182)
a. where women contribute more to subsistence than do men.
b. with polygyny.
c. that are complex, but not industrialized.
d. food-getting societies.
e. where couples live with the bride's family.

18. Which of the following has *not* been cited to support the "childhood familiarity theory of incest? (182-184)
a. the finding that Taiwanese couples who were raised together have more sexual troubles than other couples who began to live together only later.
b. the finding that children raised together on Israeli kibbutzim are uninterested in each other sexually after growing up.
c. the observation that in many domestic animals males avoid sexual relationships with females they have been brought up with.
d. the finding that American men are more likely to have sex with their daughters if they had little to do with her upbringing.

Match the term with its definition.
a. children of siblings of the opposite sex
b. marrying within one's group
c. man marries his brother's widow
d. children of siblings of the same sex
e. man marries his deceased wife's sister
f. marrying outside of one's group

19. cross cousin _____ (186)
20. exogamy _____ (186)
21. levirate _____ (187)
22. parallel cousin _____ (186)
23. endogamy _____ (186)
24. sororate _____ (187)

25. Polygyny (187)
a. is permissible in a majority of human societies.
b. is permissible only in a minority of human societies.
c. refers to the marriage of a woman to more than one husband.
d. is most common in societies with hunting technologies.
e. is most likely where men marry at an early age.

26. In which type of society is polygyny *least* likely to occur? (189-190)
a. societies where men marry at a later age.
b. societies with long post-partum sex taboos.
c. societies where men marry at a younger age.
d. societies with more women than men.
e. societies with a greater danger of kwashiorkor.

27. The polyandrous Tibetans, Toda and Sinhalese all had (190-191)
a. a shortage of women.
b. a shortage of men.
c. long post-partum sex taboos.
d. a great deal of warfare.
e. nuclear family households.

28. The *best* predictor of extended family households is (193)
a. pastoralism.
b. intensive agriculture.
c. housing shortages.

d. incompatible activity requirements of husbands or wives.
e. monogamous marriages.

Study Questions

1. Describe the marriages that occur between two males and between two females in different societies. How are they different from male-female marriages? How are they similar?

2. What are the different arguments for why marriage occurs in all human societies? Which theory is most compatible with cross-species studies?

3. Describe the different kinds of economic exchanges that take place upon marriage. What kinds of society are most likely to have bride price? Why? Which are most likely to have dowry?

4. What are the different theories for the incest taboo? What are the problems and the evidence for each?

5. How have anthropologists explained polygyny? Which theories are best supported by cross-cultural data?

6. What is the difference between matrifocal, nuclear and extended family households? How have anthropologists explained extended family households? What is the evidence?

Answers to Review Questions

1)c; 2)c; 3)a; 4)c; 5)b; 6)b; 7)d; 8)a; 9)d; 10)e; 11)b; 12)a; 13)d; 14)c; 15)a; 16)a; 17)c; 18)c; 19)a; 20)f; 21)c; 22)d; 23)b; 24)e; 25)a; 26)c; 27)a; 28)d

Chapter 11

Marital Residence and Kinship

Chapter Outline

Overview

This chapter looks at kinship groups that are larger than the immediate family. After first examining why people reside with different types of relatives after marriage, it turns to descent systems, and finally examines kinship terminologies.

I. In different societies newly married couples may live with or near different sets of relatives. 1) *Neolocal* residence (where the couples live apart from either spouse's parents) is fairly rare, occurring in about 5% of all societies. It is most common in commercial societies (like our own), where couples must often leave home to find jobs, and where they can buy what they need with money. This means that they do not need to depend on relatives for such services as baby-sitting, or borrowing money. 2) *Bilocal* residence (where couples can live with either spouse's parents) is found in 7% of the world's societies. It is most common in societies that have recently suffered depopulation, probably because this allows couples to move in with whichever spouse still has living parents. It is also common in those food-collecting societies with small bands or unpredictable low rainfall. 3) *Patrilocality* (where the couple lives with the groom's parents) is the most common form of residence, found in 67% of all societies. It is found mostly in societies with some internal warfare, probably because this ensures that related men, whose loyalties can be counted upon, will fight together. 4) *Matrilocality* (where couples live with the bride's parents) occurs in 15% of societies. It is most common in those societies without internal warfare and where women contribute more to subsistence than men. 5) *Avunculocality* (where the couple lives with the groom's mother's brother) is found in only 4% of the world's societies. This type of residence is most common in matrilineal societies that have recently begun to have internal warfare, probably because it puts loyal, matrilineally-related males together.

II. The way people calculate descent also varies from one society to another. 1) In *bilateral* kinship systems relatives on both the mother's and father's side are considered equally important. The *kindreds* thus formed are ego-centered, in that every person (except for full siblings) has a different kindred. One's kindred does not persist beyond one's lifetime, and cannot act as a corporate group. 2) In *unilineal* systems people calculate their descent through either their father or their mother, but not both. Unilineal systems have clearly defined boundaries. Every individual in a given descent group has exactly the same relatives. Such groups can own a common piece of land or act as a group to regulate marriage, perform religious rites, or make political decisions. One of the most important functions of unilineal systems is ensuring that members remain loyal to each other in battles -- cross-cultural studies show that unilineal descent groups are most common in societies with more warfare.

There are various kinds of unilineal descent groups. In *lineages* people can trace their descent from a common ancestor (or ancestress) through known links. With *clans* people assume they are descended from a common ancestor (or ancestress), but cannot trace the actual links. *Phratries* are groups composed of more than one clan. When a society is divided into only two major descent groups, these are called *moieties*. A society may contain any combination of these kinds of groups (although phratries imply the existence of clans). Societies with moieties are generally small, while those with clans and phratries tend to be larger.

Each of these different unilineal descent groups may also differ in the ways they calculate descent links. Any of them may be *patrilineal* if calculations are through male relatives only, *matrilineal* if calculations are through female relatives only, or *ambilineal* if individuals have the option of tracing their descent through either their mother or their father. How a society calculates descent is related to its marital residence pattern: Patrilineal societies are almost always patrilocal, matrilineal societies are almost always matrilocal (or avunculocal), and ambilineal societies have usually suffered depopulation and have bilocal residence.

III. Societies also differ in the words they use to refer to relatives. 1) *Omaha* kinship terminologies are most common in patrilineal societies. With this system people use the same term ("mother") to refer to all the women of their mother's patrilineage, and the same term ("mother's brother") to refer to all the men of her patrilineage. 2) *Crow* kinship terminologies are the reverse of Omaha terminologies. Crow kin terms are most likely in matrilineal societies. With this system people use the same term ("father") to refer to all the men of their father's matrilineage, and the same term ("father's sister") to refer to all the women of his matrilineage. 3) With *Iroquois* kin terms people use one term to refer to all their same-sex cross-cousins, and another term to refer to all their same-sex parallel cousins and siblings. Iroquois kinship terms are most common in societies either with unilineal descent groups in the process of developing, or in which there is a cultural preference for people to marry their cross-cousins. 4) *Sudanese* kin terms are found most often in politically complex societies with class stratification and occupational specializations. With this system all of the different kinds of cousins, aunts and uncles, nephews and nieces receive a different term. 5) With *Hawaiian* kin terms, same-sex relatives of the same generation are called by the same term. Hawaiian terms are most common in societies without unilineal descent, and with large extended families that might be composed of relatives of one's mother and one's father. 6) *Eskimo* kin terms are similar to our own. People use one term to refer to same-sex siblings, and another term to refer to all same-sex cousins. Eskimo terms are found most often in societies with bilateral kinship.

Common Misunderstandings

One of the most difficult things for students to understand is how society structures the kinds of people who are important in our lives. We often get the impression from our own society that we "choose" our own friends and other social ties. To some extent this is true, just as it is true in other societies. But there are many features of our society that encourage us to develop certain kinds of ties rather than others. In our own society we are forced to depend on professionals (who are often people we do not know well) for many services. We are also obligated to spend a good deal of our time with such categories of people as work colleagues, roommates, neighbors, and co-members of clubs or religious groups. In many senses we are just as obligated to depend on these kinds of social ties as people in other societies are forced to depend on their relatives. This chapter has attempted to explain some of the practical reasons that make societies "throw" different kinds of people together. It has also described some of the economic and emotional problems and advantages characteristic of each type of system.

Students also have trouble recognizing the importance of the fact that unilineal descent groups have clear boundaries. It is only because unilineal descent creates clear-cut groups that it is possible for a descent group to own common land, or consolidate loyalties when warfare erupts.

Key Terms and Concepts

affinal kin
ambilineal
avunculocal
bilateral
bilocal
clan
classificatory term
consanguineal kin
Crow terminology
double descent
ego-centered kin group
Eskimo terminology
Hawaiian terminology
Iroquois terminology
kindred
lineage

matriclan
matrilineal
matrilocal
moiety
neolocal
Omaha terminology
patriclan
patrilineal
patrilocal
phratry
sib
Sudanese terminology
totem
unilineal descent
unilocal residence

Review Questions

1. The post-marital residence pattern typical of American society is known as
   _____ (197)

Match the post-marital residence pattern with the definition that fits it best.
a. parents live with or near their sons and daughters-in-law
b. parents live with or near their daughters and sons-in-law
c. a couple lives away from both the groom's and the bride's relatives.
d. a couple lives with or near the groom's mother's brother.
e. a couple can live near either the bride's family or the groom's family.

2. bilocal residence _____ (197)
3. patrilocal residence _____ (197)
4. avunculocal residence _____ (197)
5. neolocal residence _____ (197)
6. matrilocal residence _____ (197)

7. Which of the following postmarital residence patterns is *least* common in
   the anthropological record? (197 198)
a. a couple lives near the groom's mother's brother.
b. a couple lives near the bride's father's sister.
c. a couple lives near the bride's parents.
d. a couple lives near the groom's parents.
e. a couple lives near neither the bride's nor the groom's family.

8. A new bride most likely to have low status or feel uncomfortable in (198)
a. a matrilocal society.
b. a patrilocal society.
c. a society with matrilineal descent.
d. a society with no internal warfare.
e. a society with nuclear family households.

9. Neolocality is most likely in societies with (199)
a. commercial economies.
b. bilateral descent.
c. high male mortality in warfare.
d. a good deal of internal warfare.
e. matrilineal descent and patrilocal residence.

10. Matrilocality is most likely in societies with (199-200)
a. matrilineal descent and nuclear family households.
b. internal warfare and matrilineal descent.
c. no internal warfare where women contribute more to subsistence.
d. large populations.
e. large populations where women contribute more to subsistence.

11. Which is most associated with patrilocal residence? (199-200)
a. warfare between communities speaking the same language.
b. ambilineal descent.
c. warfare between communities speaking different languages.
d. high male contribution to subsistence.
e. confidence that one's daughter will not marry an enemy.

12. Cross-cultural evidence suggests that bilocal societies (200)
a. generally have nuclear family households.
b. generally have larger populations than do societies with matrilocality or patrilocality.
c. may be common in hunting-and-gathering societies with small bands and unpredictable or low rainfall.
d. may result from sudden population increase.
e. are likely to characterize the future of industrial societies.

13. "Double descent" refers to a kinship system in which (202)
a. an individual affiliates for some purposes with one type of descent group and for other purposes with another type of descent group.
b. an individual belongs to a group which calculates some genealogical links through females and other links through males.
c. a female calculates her genealogy through her father and a male calculates his genealogy through his mother.
d. a female inherits her affiliation from her mother and a male from his father.
e. an individual can manipulate his or her identity at will, according to the specific circumstances.

14. Bilateral kinship is distinctive in that (204)
a. it forms clear-cut groups of kin that can act as corporate groups.
b. with this system people cannot participate in activities with kin.
c. different members of one's kin group are not relatives of each other.
d. it occurs primarily among societies with a great deal of warfare.
e. it does not allow for the development of kindreds.

15. The kinship group that is *least* likely to have a name, own property, or fight as a group is (204-206)
a. a kindred.
b. a clan.
c. a matrilineage.
d. a patrilineage.
e. a phratry.

16. Which of the following would not belong to a man's matrilineage? (204-205)
a. his mother
b. his daughter
c. his mother's brother
d. his mother's mother
e. his sister's son

17. Which of the following would not belong to a man's patrilineage? (204-205)
a. his mother
b. his daughter
c. his sister
d. his father's sister
e. his brother's daughter

18. Unlike clans, lineages (205)
a. can be either patrilineal or matrilineal.
b. are based on genealogical links that can be specified.
c. are based on kindreds.
d. are based on kin ties.
e. are also found in simpler societies.

Match the kinship group with the phrase that fits it best
a. often designated by a *totem*.
b. often designated by the name of a common ancestor or ancestress.
c. one of two such groups in a society.
d. does not form clear-cut groups.
e. must contain more than one clan.

19. kindred _____ (203)
20. phratry _____ (206)
21. clan _____ (205)
22. lineage _____ (205)
23. moiety _____ (206)

24. Among the Kapauku Papuans of Western New Guinea (207)
a. all the members of a patriclan live in the same or adjoining villages.
b. people of the same patrilineage live in the same village or in an adjoining villages.
c. the patriclan is the largest recognized group in the society.
d. members of the same patriclan do not go to war against each other.
e. members of the same patrilineage cannot marry each other, but members of the same patriclan can.

25. Unlike patrilineages, matrilineages (208)
a. are usually locally endogamous (people marry others of the same community).
b. usually do not own property as a group.
c. are almost never found together with matriclans.
d. usually give the primary leadership role of the lineage to a woman.
e. are unlikely to regulate marriage.

26. Cross-cultural studies suggest that avunculocality (209)
a. is unlikely to occur in societies with matrilineality.
b. may be a way to provide patrilineal inheritance within a matrilineage.
c. is most common in societies with kindreds and a great deal of warfare.
d. may be a way to keep males of the same matrilineage together in order to form a loyal fighting force.
e. is highly unlikely to ever occur.

27. Unilineal descent groups may do all of the following *except* (209-211)
a. manage communal property.
b. regulate marriage.
c. organize for warfare.
d. settle disputes between members.
e. form kin groups that have no boundaries.

28. Which of the following is most true? (211-212)
a. Societies with unilineal descent almost always have unilocal residence.
b. Societies with unilocal residence almost always have unilineal descent.
c. Societies with unilineal descent are more likely than those with bilateral descent to have kindreds.
d. Societies with unilineal descent are unlikely to have much warfare.
e. Unilineal descent groups cannot own communal property.

29. Which is most associated with ambilineal descent? (213)
a. bilocal residence.
b. rapid population expansion.
c. matrilocal residence.
d. patrilocal residence.
e. neolocal residence.

Match the kinship terminology with the description that fits it best.
a. one's father's sister's son is called "father"
b. one's mother's brother's daughter is called by the same term as one's mother
c. all of the different kin categories are called by a different term
d. male cross-cousins are called one term, while male parallel cousins and siblings are called another term
e. all of one's relatives of the same sex and generation are called by the same term
f. the terminological system used by most Americans

30. Iroquois System_____ (215-216)
31. Crow System _____ (215)
32. Omaha System _____ (213-214)
33. Sudanese System _____ (216)
34. Hawaiian System _____ (216)

7 7

35. Eskimo System _____ (217)

Match the kinship terminology with the type of society in which it is most likely to be found.
a. society with matrilineages.
b. society with patrilineages.
c. society with complex political system, and many specialized occupations.
d. society where people marry their cross-cousins.
e. society without unilineal descent.

36. Iroquois System_____ (215-216)
37. Crow System _____ (215)
38. Omaha System _____ (213-214)
39. Sudanese System _____ (216)
40. Hawaiian System _____ (216)

1. Discuss the different post-marital residence patterns in order, from the most common to the least common. How might these different residence patterns be explained? Can these explanations account for why some patterns are more common than others, or why here living with the bride's father's sister is so rare?

2. What do anthropologists mean by unilineal descent?   What do they mean by kindred? What advantages does unilineal descent offer to a society?

3. What are the differences between kindreds, lineages, clans, moieties and phratries? How might these differences be explained?

4. What are the different kinds of kinship terminologies anthropologists have distinguished? Describe how these terminologies are related to different types of descent systems. Explain why this is so.

Answers to Review Questions

1)neolocality; 2)e; 3)a; 4)d; 5)c; 6)b; 7)b; 8)b; 9)a; 10)c; 11)a; 12)c; 13)a; 14)c; 15)a; 16)b; 17)a; 18)b; 19)d; 20)e; 21)a; 22)b; 23)c; 24)b; 25)a; 26)d; 27)e; 28)a; 29)a; 30)d; 31)a; 32)b; 33)c; 34)e; 35)f; 36)d; 37)a; 38)b; 39)c; 40)e

Chapter 12

Associations and Interest Groups

Chapter Outline

I. Nonvoluntary associations
   A. Age-sets
      1. Karimojong age-sets
      2. Shavante age-sets
   B. Unisex associations
      1. Mae Enga Bachelor associations
      2. Ijaw women's associations

II. Voluntary associations
   A. Military associations
   B. Secret societies
   C. Regional associations
   D. Ethnic associations

III. Explaining variation in associations

Overview

This chapter is the last in a series of chapters on social ties. It examines social ties that go beyond family and kinship. These associations or interest groups are based on shared interests or goals, have some kind of formal, institutional structure and instill a sense of mutual pride and belonging. They may vary in size and form, and may be based on universally ascribed qualities, like age and sex, on variably ascribed qualities, like ethnic background, or on achieved qualities, like one's profession.

Two examples of involuntary associations based on universally ascribed qualities are age-sets and unisex associations. Among the Karimojong of East Africa and the Shavante Indians of Brazil members of a given age group pass *as a group* to the succeeding age category. The oldest *age-sets* have the greatest authority in the society, although among the Karimojong the very oldest men are eventually retired. In other societies people pass individually into new age categories. That is, they have *age-grades*, but not *age-sets*. Although Shavante females are also organized into age-sets, these sets are nowhere near as important as the men's sets. One theory for age-sets sees these groups as taking over the normal functions of kin groups in societies where kinship organization is weak. A second theory argues that age-sets become important in societies with a history of territorial rivalry, but with a lack of central authority and only dispersed kin groups. Cross-cultural evidence best supports a third theory that sees age-sets as providing needed allies in societies with frequent warfare and local groups that change in size and composition throughout the year. In such societies people need age-mates because kin are not always around to serve as allies.

The bachelors' associations of the New Guinea Mae Enga, and the southern Nigerian Ijaw women's societies are examples of nonvoluntary unisex societies. The Mae Enga bachelor's associations provide links to other villages, and display the size and magnificence of the home village to one's enemies. The associations also reaffirm a man's sense of masculinity by "protecting" the young men against the "polluting" nature of women, who in Mae Enga society often come from enemy groups. Women's participation in marketing and trade may explain the Ijaw women's societies. These societies adopt rules for proper behavior, loan money, judge breaches of norms, and carry out punishments.

Voluntary associations can be of various types. 1) Military associations like those of the Cheyenne, are joined by men and boys ready to go to war. 2) Secret societies, like the *Poro* society of Liberia and Sierra Leone, the Freemasonry of Europe, and the Ku Klux Klan of the United States often wield hidden political power. 3) Regional associations like the *serrano* associations of Lima, Peru, bring together recent urban immigrants from specific areas of the country, and provide services like lobbying central governments, and helping people adjust to their new environment. 4) Ethnic associations, like the tribal unions in Nigeria and Ghana or the friendly societies of Sierra Leone help dislocated people keep in touch with their traditional cultures, and may provide various kinds of financial assistance. 5) Other voluntary associations include: trade unions, charitable organizations, political parties, bridge clubs, churches and block associations. Although cross-cultural studies have yet to be carried out, limited evidence suggests that variably ascribed voluntary associations (like regional or ethnic organizations) may be associated with recent urban migration. Achieved voluntary organizations may be a later development as people begin to specialize in their jobs, and to emphasize achievement.

Common Misunderstandings

Students often have trouble telling the difference between an explanation and the simple giving of a name to something. Obviously, simply labelling or categorizing a phenomenon is not enough to tell us why it exists. This chapter presented various types of non-kin associations, giving descriptive "names" to each. This labelling of things is sometimes an important first step in trying to figure out what we want to explain, but social scientists want to go beyond this level. While anthropologists have studied kinship fairly thoroughly and can predict which kinds of society will have which types of kinship systems, we know fairly little about why cultures vary with regard to other forms of social organization. Except for the research cited on age-set systems, we have no systematic cross-cultural studies on other kinds of non-kin associations. There is still much to be learned about why some, but not all societies have such diverse organizations as unisex associations, regional clubs, secret societies, block associations, or religious groups.

Key Terms and Concepts

achieved qualities   interest groups
age grade   Poro
age set   serrano
ascribed qualities   tribal unions
"friendly" society   unisex association

Review Questions

1. Which of the following is *not* characteristic of all associations? (221)
a. the exclusion of some people.
b. some kind of formal, institutionalized structure.
c. a sense of belonging and pride among members.
d. members with common interests or purposes.
e. voluntary membership.

2. A variably ascribed characteristic is (221)
a. a trait acquired by doing something.
b. acquired at birth, but not found in all societies or persons.
c. based on some characteristic acquired at birth, but later modified by the individual's own activities.
d. acquired at birth and found in all societies.
e. a characteristic attributed to some people but not others based on their feelings of membership.

3. Anthropologists call a group of persons of similar age and sex who move through some or all of life's stages together (222)
a. an age-set.
b. an age term.
c. an age group.
d. an age-grade.
e. an age team.

4. Entry into an age-set is (222)
a. non-voluntary.
b. a voluntary act.
c. determined by certain achievements, like hunting a large animal.
d. an individual matter.
e. dependent upon one's ability to concentrate on life during another period.

5. If two people are called by the same term to identify their age, but were not initiated together into their new age category, we say they belong to (222)
a. the same age-set.
b. the same age-grade.
c. different age sets.
d. different age grades.
e. different voluntary associations.

6. Which does *not* characterize the Karimojong the senior generation-set (223)
a. can still recruit new members
b. consists of several age-sets
c. holds the most authority
d. is closed to new members
e. will eventually become the retired generation-set.

7. Among the Shavante Indians the members of the bachelor's age-set (223-224)
a. all receive wives on the same day, when they emerge from the bachelor's hut for the last time.

b. are the primary warriors of the community.
c. have a good deal of authority in community decision-making.
d. change their names as their members grow older.
e. stay together only during periods when the community is at peace.

8. The bachelors' associations of the Mae Enga (226)
a. are made up of unmarried men who have begun to sleep in the men's house rather than in their maternal homes.
b. are made up of men who have taken lifelong vows of celibacy in order to avoid the polluting nature of women.
c. wield a good deal of power, since the bachelors are thought of as the community's warriors.
d. are made up of all those men who sleep in the men's house.
e. help young men arrange trysts with their lovers in the forest.

9. The women's associations of the Nigerian Ijaw (226-227)
a. are composed of recently married women who use the association to adjust to their new home in their husband's village.
b. are made up of women who have passed puberty rites, but have not yet married.
c. fine members who fail to appear at meetings.
d. are composed of women who cannot support themselves through their marketing activities, and so come together to join forces.
e. are subordinate to the economically more powerful men's associations.

10. Among the Cheyenne Indians (227)
a. the military society consisted only of men who had carried out daring feats during war raids.
b. all males were required to join one of the military societies.
c. military societies were open to any man or boy willing to go to war.
d. some girls were associated with the different military societies, and provided sexual services to their men.
e. the military societies had no formal leaders, but were ruled by consensus.

11. Membership in the *Poro* societies of the Kpelle, Mende and Temne (228-229)
a. is open to all men who pass through the grueling initiation rituals of the society.
b. is required of all married men.
c. is based on political acumen.
d. is made public at a ceremony following a man's expression of a desire to enter political life.
e. is contingent on recommendations made by those already in the society.

12. An example of a secret society in the United States is (229)
a. the Ku Klux Klan.
b. fraternities.
c. the National Academy of Sciences.
d. the Church of Jesus Christ of the Latter Day Saints.
e. the cotton club.

13. An example of a "regional" association is (229-230)
a. an organization of migrants from Appalachia living in Chicago.
b. the Northeast Anthropological Association.

c. the Southern Baptist Church.
d. the Poro society as it unifies different regions in Western Africa.
e. a county government.

14. The tribal Unions of Nigeria and Ghana (230)
a. are secret societies.
b. are primarily political organizations aimed at protecting people's ancestral
   homelands.
c. were military associations organized to expel foreigner colonizers.
d. are associations of people from a same ethnic group who have moved away from
   their tribal homelands.
e. function primarily to guarantee workers' rights with regard to pay and working
   conditions.

15. Regional associations are most likely to form (229)
a. in rural areas.
b. in urban areas.
c. in pastoral societies.
d. in egalitarian societies.
e. in societies with democratic governments.

16. Unlike tribal unions, the *friendly* societies of West Africa (230)
a. limited their activities primarily to mutual aid.
b. had more peaceful aims.
c. were public organizations.
d. were urban rather than rural in origin.
e. were less interested in labor conditions and more interested in providing
   entertainment and facilitating socializing among members.

Match the society with the kind of association it has.
a. powerful secret society
b. age-sets for women
c. generation-sets.
d. association for women traders.
e. military associations

17. Ijaw _____ (226-227)
18. Shavante _____ (223-224)
19. Karimojong _____ (222-223)
20. Cheyenne _____ (227)
21. Temne _____ (228)

22. Age-sets are associated most strongly with (232-233)
a. the introduction of agriculture.
b. the breakdown of kinship ties.
c. lack of centralized authority.
d. frequent warfare, and local groups that change in size and composition
   throughout the year.
e. societies with territorial rivalry.

23. Voluntary associations are most common in (233)
a. societies with little centralized authority.

b. egalitarian societies.
c. societies with a great deal of warfare.
d. hunting and gathering societies.
e. recently urbanized societies.

24. Associations in the most highly industrialized societies apparently are becoming (233)
a. more strongly based on ethnic identities.
b. more generalized in that they provide for a multitude of different needs.
c. more based on ascribed characteristics.
d. more heavily based on geographical proximity.
e. more heavily based on achieved characteristics.

Study Questions

1. What are universally ascribed characteristics?   Variably ascribed characteristics?   Illustrate each with an example of an association that uses that particular type of membership qualification.

2. What are the differences between age-sets, age-grades and generation-sets? Describe the age-set system of the Karimojong pointing out these differences.

3. How is the bachelor's association of the Mae Enga similar to the bachelor's age-grade among the Xavante? In what ways is it different?

4. Describe the Poro society of Liberia and Sierra Leone. In what ways might this society be similar to secret societies found in the United States? In what ways might it be different?

5. What are the differences between the regional, ethnic and occupational societies found in contemporary societies? Give examples.

6. What are the theories anthropologists have proposed to explain age-sets? What is the evidence for each?

7. Give examples of associations in complex societies that are based on variably ascribed characteristics and on achieved characteristics. What are the differences between the two types of association?

Answers to Review Questions

1)e; 2)b; 3)a; 4)a; 5)b; 6)a; 7)a; 8)a; 9)c; 10)c; 11)a; 12)a; 13)a; 14)d; 15)b; 16)a; 17)d; 18)b; 19)c; 20)e; 21)a; 22)d; 23)e; 24)e

Chapter 13

Political Organization:
Social Order and Disorder

Chapter Outline

I. Variations in types of political organization
  A. Bands
  B. Tribes
    1. Kinship bonds
    2. Age-set systems
    3. Leadership
  C. Chiefdoms
  D. States
  E. Factors associated with political variation
  F. The spread of state societies

II. Resolution of conflict
  A. Peaceful resolution of conflict
    1. Community action
    2. Informal adjudication without power
    3. Ritual Reconciliation -- Apology
    4. Oaths and ordeals
    5. Codified law and the courts
  B. Violent resolution of conflict
    1. Feuding
    2. Raiding
    3. Large-scale confrontations
  C. Explaining warfare

Overview

   This chapter deals with political questions -- the ways decisions are made and conflicts resolved for territorial groups.

I. Anthropologists typically classify societies into four categories according to how they organize political decision-making. 1) In *band* level societies people live in small and usually nomadic groups. Social roles are based on age and sex, and there is equal access to prestige and resources. Leadership is based on influence acquired because of admired personal qualities. Generally bands have a hunting and gathering technology. 2) *Tribes* are also egalitarian, and informally governed, but unlike bands, they have forms of organization (like clans and age-sets) that can unite diverse communities. Among the Tiv, for example, segmentary lineages can unite various villages for warfare. Among the Karimojong, people can call upon members of their age-set for support no matter where they go. Unlike the United States, leaders in tribal societies generally do not have more wealth than their followers, and they do not govern beyond their own community, but they share many other personal characteristics--

intelligence, ambition, height and age -- with their United States counterparts. 3) *Chiefdoms* differ from tribes and bands in having a formal structure to integrate different communities. Usually there is a *chief* who rules over several communities, and who inherits his position and prestige. Chiefdoms are usually found in societies with denser populations, and more permanent settlement patterns, often with redistributive economic systems. 4) *States*, like ancient rume and the Nupe, are autonomous political units with centralized government and the power to use physical force to collect taxes, enforce laws, and draft men for work or war. States also have class stratification, intensive agriculture, and economic specialization.

Cross-culturally, the increasing complexity of political systems is associated with similar trends in technology (from hunting and gathering to horticulture to intensive food production), in population (from small nomadic groups to large permanent communities), in social stratification (from egalitarian to rank to stratified), and in economic systems (from emphasis on reciprocity, to redistribution, to commercial exchange). Yet no one factor seems to fit all the known archeological sequences culminating in state formation. Some researchers feel that the general evolutionary trend for the world to be composed of ever fewer autonomous political units will continue into the future.

II. Disputes within a society may be resolved peacefully or through violence. Peaceful ways of resolving conflict include community action (like the community decision to execute a murderer among the Eskimo). Informal adjudication without power (as in the mediator role of the Nuer "leopard-skin chief") may also solve a dispute peacefully. Still other ways of peacefully solving problems include the requirment that offenders apologize for their misdeads, such as the *soro* custom among the Fijians, the use of oaths and ordeals (for example, dipping one's hand into boiling water in order to determine guilt among the Tanala of Madagascar), and the elaboration of codified laws and courts (as among the Ashanti). One cross-cultural study showed that oaths and ordeals are most common in fairly complex societies where there are relatively well developed political institutions, but where the political officials lack power to enforce judicial decisions, perhaps because the use of the "supernatural" to pass judgment does not risk the authority of the rulers. Capital punishment is associated with *higher* homicide rates.

Violent methods of resolving disputes include crime (the use of violence within a group that normally resolves disputes peacefully), and warfare. Feuding is based on the principle that all members of a group share responsibility for vengeance. Raiding is a short term use of force to obtain goods, animals, women or some other resource, and is most common in pastoral societies. Large-scale warfare is more common in societies with intensive agriculture. Cross-cultural research suggests that people may go to war when they fear natural disasters, although war is unrelated to chronic food-shortages. Nation-states are more likely to go to war if they have formal alliances and trade more with each other. Military equality between nations, especially when preceded by a rapid military build-up, also seems to increase the likelihood of war.

Common Misunderstandings

The importance of warfare to society is often underestimated. As early chapters have shown, war may play an important role in the development of many aspects of social organization, like polygyny, post-marital residence patterns, unilineal descent groups and age-sets, besides its affects on religion, personality, or art. Yet despite its importance, people hold gross misconceptions about war. For example, many people characterize all primitive societies as being in a permanent state of war, while others adopt the opposite view -- that primitives are especially peace-loving. In fact societies vary a great deal. Among the Dani of New Guinea, warfare accounts for as many as a third of male deaths. Elsewhere, warfare causes relatively few deaths. Many people also assume that military equality decreases the likelihood of war, while cross-culturally evidence suggests just the opposite.

Key Terms and Concepts

apology	levels of political integration
band	oaths
capital punishment	ordeals
chiefdom	political life
codified law	political organization
complementary opposition	raiding
crime	segmentary lineage
feuding	state
headman	tribe
informal adjudicators	warfare

Review Questions

1. Which of the following factors is common to the political organization of all societies? (236)
a. the importance of economic well-being for leadership roles.
b. the use of formal or informal elections to establish leaders.
c. the attempt to create and maintain order.
d. the organization of a military organization.
e. the use of mediators to resolve disputes.

2. The "level of political organization" of a society refers to (236)
a. the degree to which a society has managed to avoid internal conflicts.
b. the largest territorial group in whose behalf political activities are organized.
c. the balance of power between different segments of a society.
d. the relative stability of a society's decision-making procedures.
e. the relative openness of a society's access to political office.

3. Which of the following terms does *not* refer to a society's level of political organization? (236)
a. state
b. tribe
c. hamlet

d. band
e. chiefdom

4. Which of the following is *not* characteristic of a band? (237)
a. nomadic life.
b. egalitarian society.
c. informal leadership
d. hunting and gathering economy.
e. high population density.

5. Leaders in band societies typically (237)
a. have a certain amount of power, but do not wield much influence since their decisions are discussed at length by the community.
b. are delegated a great deal of authority.
c. gain their positions through inheritance.
d. are elected to their positions.
e. gain their positions through public recognition of their personal qualities.

6. In contrast to bands, tribal societies are characterized by their (239)
a. political integration of many local communities on a permanent basis.
b. ability to organize various local groups into a temporary alliance.
c. formally elected leaders with power over more than one local group.
d. relatively limited military potential.
e. possession of various levels of formal government representation.

7. Which of the following is *not* characteristic of tribal societies? (239)
a. more sedentary than bands
b. informal leadership
c. kinship ties are relatively important
d. food-producing economy
e. economic stratification

8. The most common type of pan-tribal kinship group is (239)
a. the clan.
b. the segmentary lineage.
c. the moiety.
d. the patrilineage.
e. the phratry.

9. In a segmentary lineage system (239-240)
a. lineages occasionally split up, often siding with other lineages to fight the split-off group.
b. different groups maintain their unity over time through a series of treaties.
c. military power is highly limited by the factionalism that occurs within a lineage.
d. lineages that are genealogically close may fight each other, but will unite to fight a genealogically more distant group.
e. the different segments of a lineage tend to lose contact with each other over time, each forming a separate band.

10. Age-sets are most common in which type of society? (241)
a. tribal societies.

b. band-level societies.
c. states.
d. chiefdoms.
e. hunter-gatherers.

11. Which characteristic do leaders in tribal societies typically *not* share with United States leaders?
a. greater height than their followers
b. wealthier than their follwers
c. more ambitious than their followers
d. more intelligent than their follwers
e. older than their follwers.

12. Class stratification is most characteristic of (244)
a. tribes
b. bands
c. states
d. chiefdoms
e. ranked societies

Match the society with the description that fits it best.
a. a chief redistributes goods and coordinates labor.
b. age-set system helps to unite different local groups.
c. headman inherits position and is responsible for way band uses food resources, but may not lead in other situations.
d. segmentary lineages give a strong military advantage.
e. headman is older man, often head of a large extended family.
f. state-level society in which the king passed judgment on major crimes, and received cowrie shells as taxation.

13. Iglulik Eskimo _____ (238-239)
14. Nupe _____ (245)
15. !Kung _____ (238-239)
16. Karimojong _____ (241)
17. Tiv of Nigeria _____ (239-240)
18. Fijians _____ (242-243)

19. Over the past three thousand years the number of different political units in the world (247-248)
a. has increased.
b. has declined.
c. has varied according to the relative abundance of food in the world; less food has generally been associated with larger (but fewer) political units.
d. has remained roughly the same.
e. has varied in a periodic fashion, but with no apparent correlation with food supply.

Match the method used to resolve conflict with its name.
a. the influence of the Nuer leopard skin chief in solving disputes
b. the Eskimo consultation of all community members before deciding to execute a murderer

c. the judging of a man's guilt by requiring him to fetch a stone from a pot of boiling water, and examining his burns among the Tanala of Madagascar

d. the custom of standing in a circle and swearing to tell the truth among the Rwala Bedouins, under penalty of ruining one's descendants.

e. In the Fijian *soro* custom, the guilty person asks for forgivenss from the higher ranking offended person.

f. the examining and cross-examining of witnesses as well as parties to a dispute among the Ashanti of West Africa

20. Codified law and courts _____ (251-252)
21. Oaths _____ (251)
22. Ordeals _____ (251)
23. Informal adjudication without power _____ (250)
24. Community action _____ (249)
25. Ritual reconciliation_____ (250-251)

26. Oaths and ordeals are most likely to be found in societies (251)
a. at the state level of political organization.
b. at the band level of political organization.
c. that are somewhat complex, but where leaders have limited power, and are not willing to take responsibility for decisions.
d. with highly complex political structures and established police forces.
e. where religion plays a major part in the daily life of most of the common people, mostly as a function of the power invested in a local priesthood.

27. Comparisons of different Israeli kibbutzim suggest that courts and laws may be more likely (252)
a. where a person's actions are less visible to the public.
b. where people know each other better and so can agree on a common set of laws that all will adhere to.
c. where the people who make up a community are from similar ethnic backgrounds.
d. where the people who make up a community are from different ethnic backgrounds.
e. where people are less religious.

28. Cross-cultural evidence suggests that capital punishment (250)
a. is more likely where people depend on oaths and ordeals to determine guilt
b. is more likely where formal authorities (like courts or chiefs) have the power to punish murderers.
c. fathers are more distant from their sons.
d. social sanctions consist primarily of community action.
e. does not decrease the incidence of murder.

29. Warfare is most likely (255-256)
a. between modern nations that do not trade more with each other.
b. in societies with chronic food shortages.
c. among modern nations that do not have formal alliances with each other.
d. among modern nations that are militarily more equal.
e. in complex societies.

Study Questions

1. What political criteria distinguish *bands*, *tribes*, *chiefdoms* and *states*? What kinds of food-getting techniques, economic systems and stratification systems are correlated with each?

2. Describe the segmentary lineage system of the Tiv. What is meant by "complementary opposition"?

3. How do the Karimojong age-sets serve to organize this people politically?

4. What are some of the ways societies without formal laws or courts manage to resolve conflicts peacefully? Give examples.

5. In what kinds of society are oaths and ordeals most likely? Why?

6. In what kinds of society is warfare most likely? How might this be explained?

Answers to Review Questions

1)c; 2)b; 3)c; 4)e; 5)e; 6)b; 7)e; 8)a; 9)d; 10)a; 11)b; 12)c; 13)e; 14)f; 15)c; 16)b; 17)d; 18)a; 19)b; 20)f; 21)d; 22)c; 23)a; 24)b; 25)e; 26)c; 27)a; 28)e; 29)e

Chapter 14

Psychology and Culture

Chapter Outline

I. The universality of psychological development
   A. Early research on emotional development
   B. Recent research on cognitive development

II. Cross-cultural variation in psychological characteristics
   A. Explaining psychological variation: cultural factors
     1. Parental acceptance and rejection
     2. Task assignment
     3. Schooling
   B. Adaptational explanations
   C. Possible genetic and physiological influences
   D. Mental Illness

III. Psychological explanations of cultural variation

Overview

This chapter deals with how people think and feel in different cultures. It first examines research on possible universals of personality and cognitive development, and then turns to cross-cultural variation in personality, thought and mental illness. Finally, it looks at cultural traits that might be explained by differences in the psychological make-up of people.

I. Both Margaret Mead and Bronislaw Malinowski questioned psychological development processes once thought to be universal. Mead concluded from her field data that the "storm and stress" suffered by adolescent girls in Western societies did not occur among the Samoans. Malinowski concluded that hostility toward one's father did not occur among Trobrianders because the mother's brother was the disciplinarian, not the father. Both of these conclusions have been questioned by more recent researchers. Similarly, various psychologists have argued that people in non-Western societies do not perform as well as Westerners on measures of cognitive development, such as Piaget's tests of conservation. However, lack of familiarity with testing materials or procedures may explain these findings, since test scores of non-Westerners are the same as for Europeans when more familiar materials like earth, nuts or clay are used to measure conservation abilities. Also, Liberians actually appear to think "more abstractly" than Americans when the materials to be classified are bowls of rice rather than cards.

II. Cultures vary greatly in the ways they raise their children. This variation appears to be greater from one culture to another than within a single culture. For example, even unconventional parents in the United States resemble other Americans in that they wean their children fairly early and carry them little. Cross-culturally, there is much greater variation in these practices as well as in such customs as training for aggressiveness and attitudes toward sexuality. Those aspects of personality or thought that are typically shared by most members of a society are called modal personality characteristics. Some modal personality traits might be explained by differences in socialization. For example, cross-cultural research shows that when parents typically neglect their children, these children tend to be more hostile and aggressive. Such parental rejection may be more common where women get little relief from child care, or have little leisure time. Practical matters may also affect how much parents tolerate aggressiveness in their children: parents living in cramped quarters or extended family households are more likely to punish their children for aggressiveness. Additional evidence suggests that the kinds of tasks children are assigned to do may affect their personalities. When children must care for their younger siblings they are generally more nurturant, and when they perform tasks where adults are present, they tend to be less aggressive. Schooling also affects behavior, although most research has stressed its effects on thought. People who go to school generally perform better on tests of cognitive abilities although this may be due more to their greater familiarity with testing materials than to any development of "higher levels of thought."

Psychological characteristics are related to the ways people acquire their food. One cross-cultural studied showed that parents in agricultural and herding societies are more likely to stress obedience, while child care-takers in hunting and gathering societies are more likely to encourage individual assertiveness, probably because these personality traits are useful in obtaining food. Similarly, in societies with extended family households people are more likely to severely punish aggression. A controlled comparison among different East African societies showed that pastoralists are generally more likely to express aggressiveness openly than are agriculturalists, probably because pastoralists can more easily move away from problems if they arise, and are more likely to be involved in raids for cattle where aggressiveness is important. The way people think is also related to their food-getting technology. Hunters and gatherers are more "field-independent" than are agriculturalists, probably because this ability is needed to find game or other wild foods. In stressing compliance, agriculturalists inadvertently train their children to be less field independent.

Other psychological differences have been attributed to physiological or genetic causes. Studies of newborn Chinese, Navaho and Caucasian babies showed that Caucasians cried more easily, were harder to console and fought experimental procedures more. Although some researchers attributed these differences to genetics, it is also entirely possible that such pre-natal environmental differences as the mother's diet or blood pressure may have caused the personality differences. Studies among the Aymara of Peru suggest that the aggressiveness of these people may be due to hypoglycemia coupled with a low protein diet.

Early ethnographic accounts suggested that people in different societies suffered from different kinds of mental illnesses. Some North American Indians suffered from *wiitiko*, a disease that gave people cannibalistic urges. Malayans sometimes run *amok*, becoming destructively berserk. Greenland Eskimos suffer from *pibloktoq* an illness in which people strip themselves naked and wander across the ice. One argument sees *pibloktoq* as a manifestation of tetany, caused by a low calcium diet. Other researchers argue that illnesses like *amok* and *pibloktoq* may really be the same. The hysteria associated with each may result from the build-up of onerous social responsibilities and each ultimately subsides under ministrations of friends and relatives. Some comparisons of disturbed persons in different cultures suggest that all societies may have similar types and frequencies of psychotic behavior.

III. Some researchers argue that the typical personality traits of a society may affect primary institutions, like family organization or subsistence techniques. For example, one study argued that the motivation to achieve may affect a society's economic development. Other researchers argue that psychological characteristics affect primarily a society's secondary institutions, like religion and art. For example, one study showed that people who were taught to be obedient are more likely to enjoy games of strategy, while those trained to be responsible generally prefer games of chance. Another study argued that harsh male initiation rites may be a way for boys to resolve sex-identity conflicts in patrilocal societies where infants initially sleep exclusively with their mothers.

Common Misunderstandings

One of the great dangers in talking about the ways people think and feel in different cultures is to engage in harmful stereotyping. To avoid this, it is important to keep three things in mind. First, we should remember that although a given trait may be more common in one society than in another, this does not mean that *everyone* in that society will have that trait. When dealing with individuals it is always better to judge them on their own merits and faults, rather than on those of their culture. Second, although a culture may have some traits we consider negative, it probably also has other traits we consider positive. So it is important to look at all the traits before passing judgment. Third, and probably most important, we should try to understand *why* people in a given culture have particular psychological traits. A psychological characteristic may be perfectly suitable for life in one culture and unsuitable elsewhere. For example, field independence makes good sense in a hunting-and-gathering society, but would not be suitable for life in many agricultural societies, because it would detract from the cooperation needed for many kinds of activities. Studies (not reported in the text) show that field-independent people are less socially oriented than field dependent people. They resist the suggestions of others, look less at others' faces, and prefer to be physically more distant from others. Thus a society must "choose" which kinds of traits to emphasize. It cannot have both field-independence and close cooperation. Given these kinds of choices, there is no point in trying to label one society's psychological traits as superior or inferior to another's.

Key Terms and Concepts

amok
cognitive development
concrete operational stage
conservation
field independence
field dependence

formal operational stage
hypoglycemia
hysteria
modal personality
Oedipal complex
personality integration of culture

94

pibloktoq
pre-operational stage of development
projective test
primary institution
reversibility
secondary institution

sensorimotor stage
socialization
tetany
thematic apperception test
wiitiko psychosis

Review Questions

1. Anthropologists agree that (259)
a. people have different psychological traits in different societies.
b. the attribution of different psychological traits to different societies should not be made because this amounts to stereotyping a people.
c. the ways people think differ widely from one society to the next, but personalities are everywhere the same.
d. stereotypes resulting from casual observations on the psychological characteristics of different people are generally useful guides to psychological studies.
e. the study of different psychological traits is not a part of anthropology.

2. In her study of Samoa, Margaret Mead tried to show that (260)
a. adolescents in simpler societies typically go through a period of rebellion against their elders.
b. adolescence everywhere is a period of "storm and stress."
c. adolescent girls do not always go through a period of "storm and stress."
d. sexual repression in primitive societies is often much greater than in the American society of the 1920's.
e. greater freedom to engage in pre-marital sex is associated with a greater incidence of "storm and stress" among adolescent girls.

3. Malinowski used the example of the Trobriand Islanders to argue that (260)
a. in matrilineal societies boys feel hostility toward their mother's brothers rather than toward their fathers as envisioned in Freud's theory of the Oedipal complex.
b. the Oedipal complex is common in primitive societies as well as in more complex cultures.
c. the Trobrianders have an exaggerated Oedipal complex resulting from the custom of polygyny which, for practical reasons, often results in boys sleeping with their mothers while their fathers sleep elsewhere (with other wives).
d. patrilineal societies are less likely to suffer an Oedipal complex than are matrilineal societies.
e. the "Oedipal complex" does not exist in any society.

4. According to Piaget (261)
a. children in different societies go through different stages in their learning how to think, but within a given culture these stages are similar.
b. children are able to reverse actions mentally as soon as they can talk.

c. children within the same society, and from one society to another vary widely in the stages they go through while learning how to think.
d. children can understand the concept of conservation only if they have already gone through an earlier pre-operational stage of mental development.
e. people may learn to think in many different ways. Not everyone goes through the same stages of reasoning.

5. Studies in non-Western societies show that (262)
a. many adults do poorly on tests of conservation that children in our society perform well.
b. people in different societies sometimes do not understand the concept of conservation but do demonstrate formal operational thought considered by Piaget to come only after conservation has been understood.
c. the types of materials used in tests of conservation have little to do with research results.
d. children everywhere understand conservation by the time they can talk.
e. even in societies without formal schooling, people perform equally well in tests of formal operational thought.

6. Comparisons of "conventional" and "unconventional" parents in the United States show that (263)
a. compared to parents in other cultures, American "unconventional" parents differ little from other Americans in that they wean infants early and carry them for only short periods of time.
b. differences in child-rearing practices within the United States are often as great as those from one society to another.
c. there are virtually no differences in the "average" child-rearing techniques, but "unconventional" parents vary less from the "average" than do conventional parents.
d. "unconventional" parents typically conform more closely to what they perceive as the American norm than do other Americans who are less concerned about their "differentness."
e. unconventional parents are generally more careful and attentive to their children.

Match the culture with the child-rearing practice that characterizes it.
a. people masturbate their children regularly to pacify them.
b. children are not weaned until 5 or 6 years old.
c. children almost never see aggressive behavior and are simply carried off if they begin to indulge in aggressive acts.
d. boys are encouraged to hit their parents.
e. boys and girls are separated when they reach 7 years old.
f. young children are encouraged to engage in sex play.

7. Chenchu of India _____ (263)
8. Semai _____ (264)
9. Yanomamo Indians of Venezuela and Brazil _____ (264)
10. Chiricahua Apache _____ (264)
11. Alorese of Indonesia _____ (266)
12. Baiga of southern Asia _____ (264)

13. The term "socialization" refers to (265)
a. the training of children to enjoy the company of others in the society.
b. the development in children of behavior that conforms to cultural expectations.
c. the development in adults of the kinds of skills needed to get along with others.
d. a political program designed to increase equality in a society.
e. the development of social behaviors that deviate from cultural expectations.

14. DuBois' study of the Alorese suggested that (266)
a. leaving a child with its father, grandparent or sibling may make the child develop a more gentle personality.
b. neglectful mothering may be responsible for the development of hostile and aggressive personalities in Alorese adults.
c. stress during infancy may have made the Alorese more tolerant and trusting of each other when adults.
d. spoiling a child by indulging its desire to breastfeed whenever it wants may lead to an aggressive selfish personality in adults.
e. the habit of masturbating children creates dependent, trusting adults.

15. Cross-cultural studies show that children are most aggressive (266)
a. where mothers are indulgent about their infants' behaviors.
b. where children are raised with the help of fathers and grandparents.
c. where they are neglected and not treated affectionately.
d. in hunting and gathering societies.
e. in societies where mothers have the most free time.

16. Mothers are *least* affectionate toward their children (266)
a. in complex societies.
b. where fathers and grandparents spend more time with the children.
c. in food-collecting societies.
d. where their light workload allows them to spend less time with their children.
e. where they have more leisure time to spend on themselves.

17. Which is most closely associated with nurturant behavior in children?
a. caring for domestic animals.
b. caring for younger siblings.
c. playing with children one's own age.
d. doing household chores other than babysitting.
e. doing chores outside the home.

18. Which of the following statements is most likely to be wrong? (268-269)
a. Schooling causes children to perform less well on cognitive tests because it stifles imagination and limits sensori motor development by forcing children to remain seated for long periods of time.
b. Schooling causes children to perform better on cognitive tests because it familiarizes children with the materials used in these tests.
c. Unschooled children may score more "abstract" on a sorting test if the materials used are familiar to them.

97

d. Children who attend school may do better on certain cognitive tasks because they are accustomed to being tested.

e. Children who attend school are more likely to *want* to do well on cognitive tests.

19. Which group is *least* likely to stress obedience among children? (270)
a. herding societies
b. working class parents in America
c. agricultural societies.
d. people living in extended family households.
e. hunting and gathering societies.

20. Which children are most likely to be field-independent? (271-272)
a. American children with very strict parents.
b. children in agricultural societies.
c. children in hunting and gathering societies.
d. children in pastoral societies.
e. children who are trained to be obedient.

21. Which newborn babies are most likely to cry a lot? (272)
a. Navaho newborns
b. Chinese newborns
c. second born children
d. Caucasian newborns
e. Researchers have not been able to establish any consistent differences in infant crying among different ethnic groups or by birth order.

Match the psychological problem with the description that fits it best.
a. an Eskimo disorder in which people strip naked and wander over the ice.
b. more common in hypoglycemic Aymara men than in other Aymara men.
c. an American Indian disorder in which people have hallucinations and cannibalistic urges.
d. a Malayan disorder in which people go destructively berserk.
e. may be related to calcium deficiency in the diet.

22. pibloktoq _____ (273)
23. hysteria _____ (274)
24. aggressiveness _____ (272)
25. amok _____ (273)
26. wiitiko _____ (273)

27. An example of a primary institution that cross-cultural researchers suggest may be influenced by psychology is (275)
a. the effect of child-training for responsibility on the kinds of games people play.
b. the influence of achievement motivation on a society's economy.
c. the effect of training for aggressiveness on a preference for diagonal lines in art.
d. the influence of growing up without one's father on one's religious beliefs.
e. the tendency to neglect children in societies with extended family households.

28. Cross-cultural studies show that games of chance are most likely in societies with child-training practices that emphasize (275-276)
a. individual initiative.
b. obedience.
c. responsibility.
d. independence.
e. achievement motivation.

29. Harsh initiation ceremonies for boys at adolescence are most likely in societies with (276)
a. matrilocality in which infant boys initially sleep with their mother, their father sleeping elsewhere.
b. patrilocality in which infant boys initially sleep with their mother, their father sleeping elsewhere.
c. matrilocality in which infant boys initially sleep with their mothers and their fathers.
d. patrilocality in which infant boys initially sleep with their mothers and their fathers.
e. none of the above.

Study Questions

1. What theories about psychological universals did Mead and Malinowski question in their studies of other cultures? What did they conclude?

2. What are some of the problems in using standard psychological tests to conclude that people think differently in different societies?

3. How are the kinds of tasks children and adults do related to their personalities? What is the evidence?

4. In what ways are the kinds of tasks children and adults do related to their cognitive abilities? What is the evidence? How might this be explained?

5. What are some of the different factors that predict which people are most aggressive? In what kinds of societies were these studies carried out?

6. What are some of the explanations anthropologists have given for the different mental illnesses found in different societies? What is the evidence for each argument?

7. What are some of the secondary institutions that may be affected by child-rearing customs? What is the evidence?

Answers to Review Questions

1)a; 2)c; 3)a; 4)d; 5)a; 6)a; 7)b; 8)c; 9)d; 10)d; 11)a; 12)f; 13)b; 14)b; 15)c; 16)a; 17)b; 18)a; 19)e; 20)c; 21)d; 22)a; 23)e; 24)b; 25)d; 26)c; 27)b; 28)c; 29)b

Chapter 15

Religion and Magic

Chapter Outline

I. The universality of religion
   A. Psychological theories
   B. Sociological theories

II. Variation in religious beliefs
   A. Types of supernatural forces and beings
      1. Supernatural forces
      2. Supernatural beings
   B. The character of supernatural beings
   C. Structure or hierarchy of supernatural beings
   D. Intervention of the gods in human affairs
   E. Life after death

III. Variation in religious practice
   A. Ways to interact with the supernatural
   B. Magic
      1. Sorcery and witchcraft
   C. Types of practitioner
      1. The shaman
      2. Sorcerers and witches
      3. Mediums
      4. Priests
      5. Practitioners and social complexity

IV. Religion and adaptation
   A. Religious change as revitalization

Overview

This chapter examines cross-cultural variation in religious practices and beliefs. For some researchers, religion serves primarily psychological functions -- either satisfying the intellect, or relieving anxiety. Tyler explained animism, the belief in a dual existence for things, as stemming from intellectual speculation about such states as dreams, trances and death. Malinowski saw religion as relieving anxieties, especially anxiety over death. And psychoanalysts saw religion as resolving anxieties springing from early childhood experiences. Other researchers see religion as serving a sociological function. Durkheim argued that sacred objects, like the totems of Australian aborigines, symbolize such social groups as clans. Swanson argued that supernatural beings represent the sovereign groups in a society.

Religious beliefs vary considerably. Some societies emphasize supernatural forces like *mana* or taboo. Other societies emphasize supernatural beings of non-human origin, like gods and spirits, or of human origin like ghosts and ancestor spirits. Belief in ghosts may come about because people are reminded of deceased loved ones in everyday life, and often dream about them. Ghosts are usually close relatives and friends, not strangers. The characteristics of gods and spirits may be related to child-rearing practices. In societies where children are nurtured immediately by their parents, people expect their gods to attend immediately to their rituals. Where parents frequently punish their children, the gods are more likely to be malevolent. Other cross-cultural studies suggest that gods may represent decision-making groups. For example, in societies with many levels of decision-making, the gods also tend to be organized into different hierarchical levels with one important high god on top (monotheism). Also, ancestor worship is more likely where descent groups are important decision-making bodies. Finally, in societies with inequality, the gods are more likely to judge human morality. Perhaps this helps maintain order in such societies; perhaps it simply reflects the fact that in stratified societies decision-making groups use judges to evaluate people's actions.

Religious practices also vary. People may communicate with the supernatural through prayer, music, trance experiences induced by drugs or self-torture, preaching, litanies, simulation or feasts. Sacrifices may mirror what is socially important in a society -- human sacrifices are most common in societies with full-time craft specialists, slavery, and the corvée, that is, where human labor is especially important. Magic refers to actions that are believed to *compel* the supernaturals to act in a given way. With sorcery, people may use materials to invoke the supernatural. With witchcraft people may cause harm simply by thought or emotion alone. To some people witchcraft is a part of everyday living. Elsewhere, as in Europe and the United States during the sixteenth and seventeenth century people may go on witch hunts. Some scholars suggest that witch hunts occured during moments of political turmoil, which lead to widespread distrust and a search for scapegoats. Others suggest that hallucinogenic drugs were responsible for the visions people had of flying and other witchcraft practices. In Salem the hallucinogen may have come from spoiled rye flour; in Europe from a popular ointment. Cross-culturally witchcraft is most common in societies without judicial procedures or authorities to deal with crime and other offenses.

There are several kinds of religious practitioner. Shamans are usually part-time curers whose methods often resemble those of psychiatrists in modern societies. If a society has only one type of religious practitioner, it is likely to be a shaman. Whereas shamans may seek out their role and train for it, sorcerers and witches usually acquire their roles because other people think them destined for it. Mediums tend to be female. Priests are more likely to gain their position through inheritance or political means, and are usually full-time practitioners. Societies with social classes, agriculture, and political integration beyond the community level are more likely to have shamans, priests, mediums and sorcerers/witches.

Some religious practices may have adaptive value. For example, the Hindu belief in the sacred cow may have beneficial consequences, as it guarantees the continuity of a relatively inexpensive animal that provides traction-power, fertilizer, fuel, leather, milk and food to poor Indians. Revitalization movements, such as the religious movements of Hiawatha or Handsome Lake among the Seneca, or the Ghost dance of the Paiute helped people adjust to changing conditions. The cargo cults of Melanesia may have resulted from relative deprivation after people lost contact with Westerners and their goods.

Common Misunderstandings

Many people are so accustomed to associating religion with morality that they find it difficult to believe that in most simpler societies supernatural beings do not judge human behavior. Morality is controlled by others in the society, not by the gods. Even accusations of witchcraft for people who misbehave are uncommon in the world's simplest hunting and gathering societies.

Another common misconception is that everyone believes in God. In fact, most of the simpler societies of the world do not have a main god who reigns over humans and other supernatural beings. Early anthropologists saw this lack of a high god as an indication of undeveloped human intellectual reflection. Today most anthropologists would attribute it to differences in the social and political organization of simpler societies.

Key Terms and Concepts

ancestor spirit	polytheism
animatism	priest
animism	relative deprivation
divination	revitalization movements
ergot	shaman
ghost	simulation
god	sorcery
magic	supernatural
mana	supernatural force
medium	taboo
monotheism	witchcraft

Review Questions

1. The kinds of events that people attribute to supernatural powers (280)
a. differ greatly from one society to the next and even within the same society over time.
b. are much the same everywhere.
c. are clearly distinguishable as religion by most people.
d. are related to the climate where people live.
e. are usually dramatic incidents like volcanoes.

2. Evidence that homo sapiens of 60,000 years ago had religious beliefs comes from (280)
a. finds of special clothing for priests.
b. written references to sacred books dating back to this time.
c. finds of what appear to be religious "altars" with special sculptures.
d. evidence that people buried their dead with food, tools and other objects, possibly considered necessary in the afterlife.
e. There is no evidence of religion prior to 30,000 years ago.

3. Tyler thought that the earliest religions were characterized by (281)
a. the belief in supernatural forces.
b. the belief in a dual existence for things.
c. individual rituals.
d. human sacrifices.
e. belief in a single high god.

Match the theory about religion with the person who proposed it.
a. Religion helps relieve anxieties (especially about death) that could disrupt
   the social group.
b. Religion stems from an intellectual curiosity about phenomena like dreams.
c. Religion helps resolve inner needs and so helps people acquire maturity.
d. Religion results from the Oedipal complex.
e. It is society, not the individual that makes something sacred.

4. Freud _____ (281)
5. Tyler _____ (281)
6. Malinowski _____ (281)
7. Jung _____ (282)
8. Durkheim _____ (282)

9. The term "animatism" most nearly means (281)
a. belief in ghosts.
b. belief in supernatural forces.
c. the worship of totems.
d. belief in a dual existence of all things.
e. belief in numerous supernatural beings.

10. Which writer held the most negative view about religion? (281)
a. Tyler
b. Malinowski
c. Freud
d. Jung
e. Durkheim

11. In adapting Durkheim's view that society is the object of religious
    veneration, Swanson argued that (282)
a. gods represent the decision-making groups in a society.
b. gods personify the relationships people had with their immediate families.
c. gods serve primarily to unify people by giving their relationship an
   emotionally convincing legitimacy.
d. religion stems from the moral need to treat one's neighbors with respect.
e. our "real" contemporary religion is "consipicuous consumption."

12. If an object or person is believed to possess impersonal supernatural powers,
    it is said to have (283)
a. animism.
b. a divinatory nature.
c. ghosts.
d. mana.
e. spirits.

13. Cross-cultural research shows that ghosts (284)
a. are generally of close relatives or other people known to the person who sees them.
b. are generally thought to be dead enemies.
c. are found in only a few of the world's societies.
d. are generally thought to be very old.
e. are almost always thought to have evil intentions.

14. Worship of ancestor spirits (284)
a. is most common in societies where descent groups have important political functions.
b. is most common among the wealthy who have inherited their wealth.
c. generally involves the belief that spirits have little to do with the living.
d. is found in societies without unilineal descent groups.
e. is found mostly where people live in small nuclear family households.

15. Cross-cultural studies show that supernatural beings are most likely to be viewed as evil (285-286)
a. in societies where warfare is an everyday danger.
b. in societies suffering from debilitating epidemics.
c. in societies without a high god.
d. in societies where children receive harsh punishments.
e. in societies where people marry women from enemy groups.

16. Monotheistic religions are found (286)
a. in all societies.
b. mostly in societies with three or more levels of decision-making groups.
c. primarily in societies where everyone has say in the political decisions made by the group.
d. mostly in societies with patriarchal family structures.
e. mostly where political decisions are made by a few despotic individuals.

17. Supernatural beings are most likely to pass judgment on morality (287)
a. in simpler societies.
b. in societies where people spend more of their lives at war.
c. where leaders cannot command police forces to control the actions of their followers.
d. in societies without monotheistic religions.
e. in societies with greater inequality

Match the belief about the afterlife with the society that has this belief.
a. belief in two types of ancestor spirits -- unnamed, and named.
b. belief that the dead return to earth to be reborn.
c. belief that murderers and those who have committed suicide are burned by the sun, but that others go to the underworld where they live as they did on earth, except for a lack of sexual intercourse.
d. belief in two types of afterlife -- one of punishment, another of reward.
e. belief that the dead live at the bottom of a lake, singing and dancing.

18. Lugbara _____ (284)
19. Hindus _____ (288)
20. Zuni _____ (287)
21. Chamulas _____ (287)
22. many Christians _____ (288)

23. Human sacrifices are most likely in societies (291)
a. that do not have monotheistic religions.
b. where people generally die either as babies, or in old age.
c. with descent groups.
d. with full-time craft specialists, slavery and the corvée.
e. with small populations where everyone knows everyone else.

24. Which of the following is *not* associated with the witch hunts of sixteenth and seventeenth century Europe and the witch trials of Salem, Massachusetts? (293)
a. hallucinogenic experiences
b. political turmoil
c. condemnations of hundreds of people.
d. undermining of legitimate political procedures.
e. periods of increased wealth for most individuals.

25. Shamanistic practices are similar to those of psychiatrists in all of the following respects *except* (295-296)
a. empathetic personality.
b. naming a person's disease.
c. use of drugs, shock treatments or other dramatic cures.
d. collection of fees for services.
e. use of strictly private consultations.

26. If a society has only one type of religious practitioner, this is likely to be a (296)
a. shaman.
b. priest.
c. sorcerer.
d. medium.
e. witch.

27. In Melanesia cargo cults are found most often in societies (299)
a. that have recently had decreasing cultural contact with the West.
b. that have suffered severe exploitation by Western civilization.
c. that have acquired Western goods, but have never been in actual contact with Western people.
d. that have the simplest technologies, most distinct from Western manufactured articles.
e. that have recently come into their first contact with Western society.

Study Questions

1. Describe the different psychological and sociological theories about religion. Cite the cross-cultural evidence that supports or refutes each.

2. Compare the attitudes of Freud, Malinowski, Jung, Durkheim and Wallace with regard to religion. What does each imply about the future of religion? Which are most positive? Which most negative?

3. What is the evidence that gods represent political (decision-making) groups?

4. In what kinds of society are people most likely to believe in witches? What is the evidence?

5. In what ways are shamans like psychiatrists in our own society? In what ways are they different?

6. What are some of the different kinds of religious practitioners found in different societies? Which kinds of societies are likely to have each type of practitioner?

7. Compare the religious movements of the Seneca with the cargo cults of Melanesia. In what ways are these movements similar? In what ways different? What might explain this?

Answers to Review Questions

1)a; 2)d; 3)b; 4)d; 5)b; 6)a; 7)c; 8)e; 9)b; 10)c; 11)a; 12)d; 13)a; 14)a; 15)d; 16)b; 17)e; 18)a; 19)b; 20)e; 21)c; 22)d; 23)d; 24)e; 25)e; 26)a; 27)a

Chapter 16

The Arts

Chapter Outline

I. Body decoration and adornment

II. Explaining variation in expressive culture
   A. Visual art
   B. Music
   C. Folklore

Overview

This chapter looks at cultural variation in body adornments, visual arts, music, and folklore.

Body decorations are used in different societies for esthetic and erotic reasons, and to denote social position. They may be permanent, as in scarification, piercing or tattoos, or may be temporary as in body-painting.

Many social scientists feel that elements of expressive culture reflect other aspects of people's lives. Even when using the same materials to fashion their artistic works, different societies vary in the things they wish to represent and the styles of their designs. This variation may reflect a group's social organization. For example, in the Middle Ages, people represented religious scenes. The ancient Sumerians portrayed their leaders as much larger and with bigger eyes than other people. Stylistically, in egalitarian societies people enjoy repeating similar elements in designs, perhaps reflecting the fact that people are similar in the kinds of tasks they perform. They also like to leave large spaces in their designs, possibly in imitation of the geographical separation between their villages. Finally, they also prefer symmetrical designs, a likely result of their equal treatment of each other. In contrast, people in stratified societies generally do not repeat the same design elements, do not leave spaces, and do not make designs symmetrical.

Music may similarly reflect the way people live. Simpler societies are more likely to have nonsense words in their songs, possibly because they have less need to communicate instructions. Societies with informal leadership are more likely to have an interlocked style of singing in which each person sings independently within the group, reflecting in song the way leadership works in life. Rank societies are more likely to have leaders begin a song, but to have the leaders soon drowned out by the others. Slightly stratified societies are more likely to have a clear-cut role for the leader, and secondary "answering" roles for the others, and highly stratified societies have soloist positions. Other aspects of society are also reflected in music. Polyphony is found most often in societies where women contribute more to subsistence, perhaps reflecting the interdependence of men's and women's tasks. A good choral blend is most likely where people must cooperate closely in the kinds of work they do.

Child-care practices may also affect musical tastes. People like music with regular rhythms where, as infants, they were carried close to their mother's body and learned to enjoy her regular walking rhythm. People tend to sing in a wider vocal range and to place firmer accents on beats when they were stressed more as infants, giving them more exploratory and bolder personalities. Where child-rearing practices stress obedience, people tend to sing more cohesively; where they stress assertiveness, people sing with raspier voices; and where they are sexually restrictive, people sing in more nasal tones.

Most research on folktales has concentrated either on universal themes or on particular cultures. For example, Kluckhohn suggested that the themes of catastrophe, slaying of monsters, incest, sibling rivalry, and castration are universal. Some scholars have attempted to reduce regional folktales to a particular version of one tale or another. Many interpretations of folktales are as fanciful as the tales themselves, and have not been tested with more systematic data. One study that tried to predict cross-cultural variation in folktales, found that where children are severely punished for aggression, their folktales are more likely to have intense aggression. Another study found that unprovoked aggression is most common in the folktales of societies with unpredictable food shortages.

Common Misunderstandings

When questioned about art, people often react in one of two ways. Some argue for the superiority of one type of art over another. Others argue that "there is no disputing tastes." Neither of these two reactions is particularly helpful for anthropology. Those who see some art forms as superior get into trouble when people disagree about just what forms of art are best. For example, American high schools often leave students with the impression that "classical" music is somehow inherently superior to other forms of music. Yet in other societies, like China during the Cultural Revolution, or the Ayatollah's Iran, this music was thought particularly degrading and was banned. Egalitarian societies often prefer music that many in our society would find terribly boring. In short, there is no clear criterion on how to judge what forms of art are best.

The argument that "there is no disputing tastes" is also problematic, because it assumes that the arts are unrelated to other aspects of people's lives. As this chapter should make clear, many aspects of a group's art reflect its social structure or child-rearing practices. Still, from what we know, art does not appear to *affect* other aspects of a culture so much as *reflect* them, so there is no reason to try to institute social reforms by prohibiting people from enjoying the kinds of art that most appeal to them.

Key Terms and Concepts

acquired reward value
art
choral blend
counterpoint
expressive culture

folklore
"interlocked" singing
polyphony
symmetry

Review Questions

1. Everywhere in the world, art (303)
a. is used to express feelings and ideas.
b. has political ends.
c. is used to decorate houses.
d. is valued for its originality.
e. techniques are passed along from specialists to their apprentices.

2. For anthropologists the term "art" refers to (303)
a. the expression of feelings and ideas in the visual arts, music, dance and folklore.
b. the ways people in a given society express their ethnic or cultural unity.
c. the work of specialists in graphic design, music, or dance.
d. the kinds of music, graphic work, dance and folklore that people regard as "serious" rather than simply decorative.
e. all forms of expressive culture, including music, graphic designs, sports, religious beliefs, rituals, popular sayings, and such reflections of personality as aggressiveness or sexuality.

3. One form of expressive behavior apparently found everywhere is (303)
a. body decoration.
b. dancing.
c. graphic representations of animals
d. theatre.
e. rhymed poetry.

4. One society where women scarified their loins and upper thighs in order to make themselves more sexually attractive was (304)
a. the Ila of Zambia.
b. seventeenth century Europe.
c. the nineteenth century English.
d. the aristocracy in Korea.
e. rural Iraq.

5. Anthropologists generally feel that (305)
a. art is thought unimportant by most people of the world, and so of little theoretical interest.
b. since art has no serious consequences for other aspects of life, it changes easily and arbitrarily, with little connection to other aspects of life.
c. art has a major influence on other aspects of people's lives, including the ways they get their food.
d. art reflects the way people live in their society.
e. art is the key to understanding other cultures.

6. Which of the following artistic styles is *least* likely to be found in an the graphic designs of an egalitarian society? (307-308)
a. much "irrelevant" space.
b. realistic representations of people.
c. repetition of simple elements.
d. symmetrical design.
e. unenclosed figures.

7. The designs painted on vases in ancient Greece (308)
a. became progressively more asymmetrical as Athens became more stratified.
b. show more artistic effort going into the designs in the those periods when Athens was more egalitarian.
c. became less crowded as Athens grew more stratified, reflecting the more refined tastes of the elite.
d. became progressively more elegant in the ways design elements were carefully set apart from each other.
e. changed little over time, despite major changes in political organization.

8. Which of the following is most likely to be found in the music of a predominately hunting society? (309)
a. the giving of many soloist parts to different band members during singing.
b. songs without words.
c. an "answering" type of singing in which a leader sings something and then is answered by the rest.
d. polyphony
e. singing in a nasalized voice.

9. Polyphony is most likely in societies (309)
a. where religion plays a greater part in people's lives.
b. with complex political systems.
c. where women contribute more to subsistence.
d. where people must work closely together coordinating their efforts with each other.
e. where men dominate in ritual life.

10. A good choral blend is most easily achieved (310)
a. in societies with professional actors or singers.
b. in societies with cohesive work parties.
c. in hunting and gathering societies.
d. in stratified societies.
e. in societies where youngsters are trained for assertiveness.

11. In societies where infants receive stress people generally sing (310)
a. in timid, faltering voices.
b. with weaker accents on the beats.
c. using a wider vocal range.
d. within a narrow vocal range.
e. in a more nasal tone.

Match the musical style with the social feature most closely associated with it.
a. greater sexual repression.
b. children are carried in close bodily contact with their mother.
c. children trained to be assertive.
d. elaborate social stratification.
e. people commonly form close work groups.

12. people sing with a raspy voice. _____ (311)
13. cohesive singing _____ (310)
14. people sing in a nasal voice _____ (311)

110

15. frequent solo parts _____ (309)
16. regular rhythms in music _____ (310)

17. Kluckhohn thought all of the following themes were found in the folklore of all societies *except* (312)
a. sibling rivalry.
b. slaying of monsters.
c. unrequited love.
d. castration.
e. catastrophe.

18. One cross-cultural study showed that intensely aggressive folktales are most likely in societies (314)
a. where children are severely punished for aggression.
b. in disequilibrium.
c. with no peaceful means for resolving disputes.
d. with professional armies.
e. with a great deal of warfare.

19. Arbitrary unprovoked aggression is most likely in the folktales of societies with (314)
a. unpredictable food shortages.
b. lax child-rearing techniques.
c. despotic rulers.
d. histories of plague.
e. human sacrifice.

Study Questions

1. What do anthropologists mean by "expressive culture?" What kinds of activities in American society would be included? Are there forms of expressive culture found in other societies that are uncommon or non-existent in the United States?

2. Describe some of the ways people adorn their bodies in different cultures. Can you think of an explanation for why societies stress different kinds of body decorations?

3. How are artistic styles and content related to social organization? What is the evidence?

4. How are elements of musical style related to social organization? How are they related to child-rearing practices?

5. What are some of the questions regarding folktales that are left unanswered by studies that attempt to reconstruct the original tales that gave rise to all the variants found in a given region? How might these other questions be examined?

Answers to Review Questions

1)a; 2)a; 3)a; 4)a; 5)d; 6)b; 7)a; 8)b; 9)c; 10)b; 11)c; 12)c; 13)e; 14)a; 15)d; 16)b; 17)c; 18)a; 19)a

Culture Change

Chapter Outline

Overview

This chapter examines why cultures always change. Sometimes cultural transformations come about through internal means, like discoveries, inventions or rebellions. Other times they come about through external influences as in diffusion or acculturation.

Discoveries and inventions include both objects and abstract phenomena like forms of social organization or religion. They may come about unconsciously (for example, the wheel may have been invented after observing children playing with fallen logs), or consciously, through deliberate attempts to invent something new (for example, the invention of the spinning jenny). A few studies suggest that the people most likely to first adopt innovations are either the wealthy (who can afford the risk), or the poor (who have nothing to lose).

Diffusion refers to the transmission of traits from one culture to another, and may occur through direct contact (for example, the importation of Chinese paper productions into different regions of the world, or the introduction of New World tobacco into Europe). Diffusion may also occur through intermediate contact (for example, the exchange of traits between Moslem and Christian countries via soldados, during the Crusades). Stimulus diffusion refers to the development of a local equivalent of a foreign trait (for example, the adoption by the Cherokee of a syllabic writing system after discovering how Europeans wrote down their languages). No matter how diffusion takes place, it is always selective -- only those traits that fit in with a society's culture are likely to be borrowed, and even those traits that are accepted are likely to be modified to fit the adopting culture.

Rebellion and revolt bring about other changes. These may be internally influenced, but still involve foreign intervention, as in the American revolution. Some conditions that may give rise to revolts include a) the loss of prestige of established authorities, b)   threats to economic improvement, c) indecisiveness of government, and d)   loss of support of intellectuals. A worldwide survey suggests that rebellions and revolts are most likely where the ruling elites depend on land, rather than capital, for their income. In such cases the elites are unwilling to give in to peasant demands, because this would more seriously endanger their wealth and power. Thus, peasants are forced to turn to violence to get what they want.

Acculturation refers to the passing of traits from a more powerful society to a weaker one. Some groups may actually want to adopt the dominant society's traits, as in the accepting of snowmobiles by Eskimos and Lapps. But more often than not, acculturation is forced on people -- for example,the forced conversion of Mexican Indians to Catholicism after the Spanish conquest, or the requirement that American Indian children go to school. In many cases groups in contact with powerful societies were simply murdered, or became extinct because of imported diseases.

Even before Western expansion, commercialization was forced on people by such dominant cultures as the Chinese, Persians, Greeks, Romans, Arabs, Phoenicians and Hindus. Contemporary studies of Western commercialization suggest that previously non-commercial peoples often turn to buying and selling goods because their lands are so reduced in size that they can no longer subsist on their own produce. One way commercialization occurs is when some members of the community move off to a nearby place to work for wages, as happened on Tikopia. Such commercialization may change a group by individualizing land ownership and household organization. Another road to commercialization occurs when groups exploit the wild products in their environment, as when the Mundurucū Indians began tapping wild rubber trees, or the Montagnais Indians began trapping animals for fur. In these cases people also shifted from a village-oriented life with cooperative labor, to a dispersed settlement pattern with individualized economic activities. Still other groups may begin commercialization by planting supplementary cash crops. In this case previously autonomous groups change into peasants, and generally become more profit and cash oriented. With a change to commercial agriculture, all the cultivated commodities are produced for sale rather than consumption. This change may involve increased mechanization, and increased social and economic differences between farmer-owners and paid laborers. Sometimes such a change may lower a group's standard of living, as in the case of Brazilian northeasterners who converted their lands to sisal production.

Groups also often change their religion. As suggested by the Tikopian case, various practical factors may have facilitated the introduction of Christianity into some groups. As illustrated by the Handsome Lake cult among the Seneca, sometimes religious movements can help people adapt to changing conditions by proposing codes of behavior more in line with the new ways of life. Too often, missionary activity tends to destroy a society's culture and self-respect by stressing sin and guilt, by using black to represent evil, and by showing hostility to native religions.

Common Misunderstandings

Many people attempt to explain a given social characteristic by pointing out that it came from elsewhere. As the text makes clear, diffusionist explanations are not very satisfying, because they fail to explain why only some cultural traits are diffused, but not others. For example, many aspects of American culture have been widely diffused abroad (such as rock music and Hollywood films), but other aspects have had less acceptance (for example, Broadway tunes, or football). It is because new traits must fit in with the rest of the culture that diffusion is selective. To explain diffusion, we must examine how these traits are integrated into a new culture. This requires explaining how the acceptance of new traits or technologies into a culture affects other aspects of people's lives.

Another common error is to imagine that change in other cultures comes about exclusively because of external influences. Popular accounts of recently contacted societies often like to claim that the cultures have remained unchanged for thousands of years, simply because they have not had contact. Others like to attribute any change (such as a new invention or a rebellion) to the meddling of outsiders. Actually, we know that most cultures are always changing, so the "thousand-years-old" claims are dubious. And, as the textbook points out, some innovations or rebellions may have internal, rather than external causes.

Key Terms and Concepts

accidental juxtaposition	industrialized agriculture
acculturation	intentional innovation
capitães	revitalization
cash crops	stimulus diffusion
commercial agriculture	unconscious invention

Review Questions

1. Compared to today, inventions in prehistoric times (317)
a. probably resulted more often from accidental juxtapositions.
b. probably resulted more often from intentional innovations.
c. were probably more common, since there were more things yet to be invented.
d. probably came about more because of stimulus diffusion.
e. were probably the work of single individuals rather than research teams.

2. One argument that could *not* explain why it took so many years for humans to invent the wheel is that (317)
a. early humans had little need of a wheel.

b. prehistoric humans were not as intelligent as modern humans.

c. early humans had more limited means of storing and accumulating knowledge.

d. modern humans invent things faster because we can accumulate knowledge through libraries and better communication systems.

e. It did not take many years for humans to invent the wheel.

3. Compared to early times, innovations today (318)

a. are less likely to affect our political organization.

b. are less likely to affect the basis of our social organization.

c. occur more rapidly.

d. occur more slowly.

e. are less sought after.

4. Research shows which group is *least* likely to innovate? (318)

a. middle-level Ashanti woodcarvers.

b. the wealthiest Ashanti woodcarvers.

c. wealthier farmers.

d. the poorest Ashanti woodcarvers.

e. lower middle class individuals.

5. The process by which cultural elements pass from one society into another is called (319)

a. acculturation.

b. innovation.

c. diffusion.

d. revitalization.

e. accidental juxtaposition.

6. Which of the following is an example of diffusion by direct contact? (320)

a. adoption of clothing in Pacific Islands.

b. adoption of paper in Europe.

c. adoption of civil service exams in Japan.

d. adoption of semitic alphabet in Greece.

e. drinking of wine in Moslem countries.

7. The adoption of the alphabet in Greece was due to (320)

a. unconscious invention.

b. intentional innovation.

c. diffusion by direct contact.

d. stimulus diffusion.

e. diffusion by intermediate contact.

8. The development of a Cherokee syllabic writing system is an example of (320)

a. unconscious invention.

b. intentional innovation.

c. diffusion by direct contact.

d. stimulus diffusion.

e. diffusion by intermediate contact.

9. The failure of Moslem societies to adopt wine drinking, gambling, playing cards and printing shows that (321)

a. societies are selective about the traits they adopt from other societies.

b. religion is the main reason cultures reject change.

c. most people have little control over which traits diffuse into their culture.

d. Moslems are especially resistant to all kinds of change.

e. cultures are usually highly resistant to change.

10. One of the reasons Indian women of northwestern California never adopted the short hair styles of the 1920's is that (321)

a. these Indians associated short hair with a sexual promiscuity that was repugnant to them.

b. these Indians were in conflict with American society at the time, and determined to demonstrate their uniqueness.

c. the short hair style never reached California.

d. these Indians looked on short hair as a symbol of mourning.

e. Indian women were proud of their ability to grow beautiful long hair which Whites could not do.

11. Which revolt was the least affected by foreign intervention? (322)

a. the French Revolution

b. the American Revolution

c. the Spanish civil war.

d. the 1948 rebellion in Czechoslovakia

e. the 1973 revolt against Chilean President Allende.

12. A worldwide study of developing countries shows that rebellions and revolts are most likely where (323-324)

a. the ruling class gains most of its income from the land.

b. rulers are indecisive about their policies.

c. people are poorest.

d. the interests of U.S. multinationals are most threatened.

e. people see their neighbors grow richer, while they themselves fail to improve.

13. In contrast to diffusion, acculturation involves (324)

a. the borrowing of traits under pressure from a more powerful society.

b. the spreading of traits from a subordinate culture into a dominant one.

c. the changing of a culture due to internal mechanisms for change.

d. the borrowing of non-material items like religions or ideologies, rather than material goods.

e. peaceful contact between groups that are more equal in power.

14. The example of the Yahi Indians, as described by Ishi (325)

a. shows that schools had a major effect on transforming many native American Indians into U.S. citizens.

b. shows that Indians often welcomed American technologies and values.

c. shows that Indians accepted many White American values, like pacifism, but rejected the White's technological "miracles."

d. demonstrates the devastating effects of disease and warfare after contact with White society.

e. shows how native American societies can expand their cultural influence.

15. Cultural contacts involving greater dependence on commercial exchange (325-326)
a. occur today, but also occurred in other periods of human history as with Chinese, Persian, Greek, Arab and Phoenician traders.
b. are a relatively new development in human history.
c. are usually sought out by relatively isolated peoples in order to acquire more goods.
d. usually result in decreased work loads for the people who produce materials for exchange.
e. usually result in dramatic increases in the quality of life for all concerned.

Match the culture with the form of commercialization it adopted.
a. people exploit wild resources for sale
b. laborers migrate to other areas for work
c. people give up growing their own food in order to grow sisal for sale
d. people begin to grow supplementary crops like coffee and wheat for sale
e. early state society that pushed commercial enterprises in other areas

16. northeast Brazilians _____ (330)
17. Tikopians _____ (326)
18. Mundurucú Indians of Brazil _____ (326-327)
19. Arusho of East Africa _____ (329)
20. Phoenicians _____ (326)

21. People who produce food for their own subsistence but also sell their surplus to others living in cities are called (328)
a. farmers.
b. horticulturalists.
c. industrial agriculturalists.
d. peasants.
e. migratory laborers.

22. Which of the following does *not* generally characterize commercial agriculture? (329-330)
a. more land becomes available for small farmers.
b. laborers migrate to urban centers in search of employment.
c. the economic gap between farm owners and farm workers increases.
d. manufactured items are introduced into rural areas.
e. living standards decline for the rural populations.

23. Which of the following is *least* likely to explain why the Tikopians converted to Christianity? (330-332)
a. People discovered that the Christian mission's teaching people how to read and write led to social and economic advancement.
b. An epidemic killed large numbers of people, including religious leaders of the native faith.
c. Tikopians already felt that their gods' influence applied only to Tikopia, and that people left their native gods behind when they left their island.
d. Chiefs often brought over their entire kin group when they converted.
e. Christianity was better able to maintain population within the limits imposed by life on an island.

Study Questions

1. What do anthropologists mean by "accidental juxtaposition" and "intentional innovation? Give examples of each. Which are most likely to have been responsible for such inventions as control of fire, the wheel, manioc processing techniques, the printing press, or firearms? Justify your response.

2. What are the differences between stimulus diffusion and intentional innovation? Give examples.

3. Examine a trait that diffused into a culture from elsewhere, and describe its effects on other aspects of the recipient group's culture.

4. Describe the ways commercialization enters previously isolated communities. What kinds of commercialization are likely to be introduced first? What kinds last?

5. Compare the Tikopian conversion to Christianity, the Seneca Indians' revitalization movement, and Melanesian cargo cults. How might the different kinds of religious movement be related to differences in the types of contact experienced by these groups? To what extent might they be related to differences in the pre-contact cultures of these peoples?

Answers to Review Questions

1)a; 2)b; 3)c; 4)a; 5)c; 6)b; 7)e; 8)d; 9)a; 10)d; 11)a; 12)a; 13)a; 14)d; 15)a; 16)c; 17)b; 18)a; 19)d; 20)e; 21)d; 22)a; 23)e

Applied Anthropology

Chapter Outline

Overview

Applied anthropology deals with planned change. Many people question whether anthropologists should engage in applied research. This is because applied anthropology has often been associated with colonialism, especially in Great Britain where anthropologists were often called upon to help in the administration of Britain's colonies. During some periods a limited labor market gave anthropologists no choice but to seek jobs outside of universities and museums. During World War II many anthropologists worked for the war effort, examining such questions as why Japanese soldiers attempted to kill themselves rather than be taken prisoner. After World War II most anthropologists returned to universities, although in recent years the declining academic market has forced many to return to applied work. Some anthropologists feel it is not right to interfere in the lives of others, but others argue that it is unethical *not* to participate in programs of planned change.

One of the problems applied anthropologists face is determining whether a planned change will truly benefit the target population. As an example of a planned change that had negative effects, a health care program once attempted to keep pregnant West African women away rom their gardening work. As a result, women's health, and infant mortality actually worsened. Irrigation projects, such as that in Sudan, often lowered the quality of people's lives by introducing diseases like bilharziasis into the population.

Even if a planned change is judged truly beneficial to a population, there may still be problems in introducing the change. People may resist a planned change for cultural, social or psychological reasons. For example, they may misinterpret the symbols used to communicate the necessity of the change, or they may feel the change runs counter to certain religious beliefs, or will interfere with their family and kin relationships. Sometimes they resist change because earlier personal experiences have made them dislike foreigners. Often the resistance of the target population may be grounded in the sound recognition that the proposed change will not be beneficial (as in the resistance of Venezuelan mothers to accept powdered milk.) Many times serious mistakes can be avoided by paying more attention to local customs and beliefs. For example, Iranian men refused to use shower baths constructed like American men's gymnasium showers because they did not like to be seen naked in front of other men. It would have been easy to construct the shower baths with partitions more in line with the local customs.

Agents of change must take into account their relations with various sets of people. They can usually achieve better results if they gain the approval and support of the local leaders. They must also deal with the administrative hierarchy of the government agency or private organization implementing the change. Finally, they must be aware of the problems that can be created by other social groups involved, such as the privileged classes who may feel threatened by the project.

One planned change in which anthropologists played an important role was the Vicos project. In this project, Cornell University took over the role of *patrón* in a Peruvian *hacienda*. From the beginning, the anthropologists gave the Indian leaders on the hacienda supervisory positions and a role in planning changes. They also abolished unpaid services, and reinvested profits into community improvements. Ten years after the project began the Indians had improved their diets, lived in better houses, and succeeded in buying the hacienda. The only negative aspect of the change was a somewhat increased psychological stress among male heads of household..

Common Misunderstandings

Many people feel that the main role of an anthropologist should be to help a minority group somewhere in the world. As this chapter demonstrates, there are cases where anthropologists have undertaken just such kinds of tasks (for example, the Vicos project). But this kind of work is actually very rare in anthropology, even in applied anthropology. More commonly applied anthropologists limit themselves to a consulting role. They may, for example, provide reports to the World Bank or government agencies on the social impacts of such activities as the construction of hydroelectric dams, irrigation works, road-building projects, slum removals, or the handling of war or famine refugees.

Of course many anthropological studies have little or no effect on the people investigated. These studies are carried out primarily to draw general conclusions about human behavior that might be useful in our own society. Students should be aware that anthropological studies can be useful at various different levels and for different groups of people.

Key Terms and Concepts

applied anthropology	patron
bilharziasis	target population
hacienda	Vicos project

Review Questions

1. Applied anthropology is most likely to be accepted by anthropologists (338)
   a. when it requires work in distant, unfamiliar cultures.
   b. when it is not associated with colonialism.
   c. when it involves work with the more privileged members of a society.
   d. when the academic job market for anthropologists is good.
   e. when it is carried out on a voluntary basis, rather than as a job.

2. In which country are anthropologists more likely to be employed by government agencies rather than by universities or museums? (338)
   a. the United States
   b. the United Kingdom
   c. Mexico
   d. France
   e. Anthropologists are more likely to have jobs in universities in all of these countries.

3. During which period of U.S. history was applied anthropology most common? (338-339)
   a. between World War I and World War II.
   b. prior to World War I.
   c. during the 1950's
   d. during World War II.
   e. during the 1960's

4. Anthropologists were asked to help the United States during World War II to (338)
   a. provide scientific data to counter the Nazi claims of the genetic superiority of "Aryans."
   b. help discover ways to mitigate the social problems resulting from repeated bombing raids on European cities.
   c. discover ways to encourage American men to sign up for the military.
   d. figure out why Japanese soldiers committed suicide rather than let themselves be taken prisoner.
   e. assess the effects of women's factory work on home life.

5. Compared to early periods, applied anthropologists in England and the U.S. today (339)
   a. concentrate more on military questions.
   b. concentrate more on political questions.
   c. concentrate less on economic questions.
   d. concentrate more on health questions.
   e. concentrate less on educational questions.

6. The code of ethics adopted by the Society for Applied Anthropology specifies that (340)
   a. anthropologists should involve the target community as much as possible in formulation of policy.
   b. anthropologists should not do research on an applied question unless formally requested to do so by the people affected.

c. anthropologists should participate in projects even if they feel they will not benefit the target community, because they can at least mitigate the problems.
d. anthropologists should report the names of all informants to ensure that their conclusions can be verified.
e. anthropologists have the right to interview any individual who consents to be interviewed.

Match the problem with the introduced social change that caused it.
a. pregnant women encouraged not to work in the fields.
b. government sprayed DDT to eliminate malaria.
c. cash crops were introduced.
d. irrigation canals were constructed.

7. an increase in the disease, bilharziasis (341)
8. increase in infant mortality (341)
9. a disastrous population explosion (341)
10. the loss of musical entertainment for work groups (341)

11. One readily adopted implemented change was the acceptance of (342)
a. hybrid corn among Spanish-American farmers in Arizona.
b. powdered milk by Venezuelan mothers.
c. seedling orchard trees by Colombian farmers.
d. family planning methods by Taiwanese women.
e. hospitalization by the Zulu.

12. The failure to understand symbols in development projects is illustrated by the example of (343)
a. the playing of the American national anthem at Olympic events.
b. the burning of American flags in Iran.
c. the use of naked lightbulbs to symbolize poverty in England.
d. the use of clasped hands to represent friendship in Thailand.
e. the use of country music to promote abortion in the Old South.

Match the problem encountered in introducing change with the country where it was found.
a. poor people fail to be interested in a product because it was advertised with a picture of a family dining by candlelight.
b. farmers fail to adopt a variety of corn because it is too hard to grind.
c. family cannot hospitalize someone without everyone's consent.
d. man refuses to permit hospitalization of his daughter because this would amount to admitting she was a witch.
e. many farmers ignore worthwhile proposed changes because the government officials that promote them are thought aloof and unlikable.

13. India _____ (345)
14. England _____ (344)
15. Spanish Americans _____ (342)
16. Zulu _____ (344)
17. Navaho _____ (345)

18. The refusal of Venezuelan women to adopt powdered milk for infants is probably an example of (345)
a. cultural resistance.
b. psychological resistance.
c. resistance due to a correct perception that powdered milk was not worthwhile.
d. religious resistance.
e. a communication problem due to misinterpreted symbols.

19. Which of the following most demonstrates an ethnocentric attitude toward implemented change? (346)
a. the involving of the target population in planning change.
b. the use of a local priest's influence to convince people to accept vaccinations.
c. working with local administrators in implementing change.
d. the promoting of new foods on a society, without first examining the nutritional contents and other aspects of native foods.
e. asking people to meet together to hash over problems.

20. The Vicos project is an example of (348-349)
a. a successful project run by anthropologists.
b. a development project that included anthropologists and failed miserably.
c. questionable anthropological ethics during the Vietnam war.
d. how grant administration can impede the work of a development project.
e. how projects that do not use anthropologists as consultants often fail to achieve their goals.

21. One of the first acts of Cornell University anthropologists after leasing a *hacienda* in highland Peru was to (348-349)
a. give the Indian agricultural workers supervisory positions and a role in planning.
b. dismiss most of the agricultural laborers on the estate because of corruption.
c. sue the Peruvian government for corruption.
d. introduce technologically more complex farming machinery.
e. seek the advice of nearby landowners regarding how to handle such an enterprise.

Study Questions

1. Why have anthropologists sometimes disapproved of applied anthropology? In what periods of history was applied anthropology most acceptable? Why?

2. What are some of the items of the code of ethics devised by the Society for Applied Anthropology? Why are these items formalized?

3. What are some of the factors anthropologists should examine before deciding to participate in an applied project?

4. What are some of the examples of how planners have used symbols that local populations misunderstood?

5. Give examples of cases where the local populations were right to reject an attempt to implement change. What does this imply about the implementation of the knowledge of anthropologists and other planners?

6. Describe the Vicos project. How successful was it? How might anthropologists profit from this experience in other attempts to implement change?

Answers to Review Questions

1)b; 2)c; 3)d; 4)d; 5)d; 6)a; 7)d; 8)a; 9)b; 10)c; 11)d; 12)d; 13)e; 14)a; 15)b; 16)d; 17)c; 18)c; 19)d; 20)a; 21)a